Psychopedagogy

Psychopedagogy

Freud, Lacan, and the Psychoanalytic Theory of Education

K. Daniel Cho

palgrave
macmillan

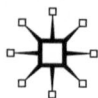

PSYCHOPEDAGOGY

Copyright © K. Daniel Cho, 2009.

First published in 2009 by PALGRAVE MACMILLAN® in the United States – a division of St. Martin's Press LLC, 175 Fifth Avenue, New York, NY 10010.

Permission to reprint:
"*Wo es war:* Psychoanalysis, Marxism, and Subjectivity," *Educational Philosophy and Theory* 39, no. 7 (2007): 703–719.
"Teaching Abjection: A Response to the War on Terror," *Teaching Education* 16, no. 2 (2005): 103–115.
"Lessons of Love: Psychoanalysis and Teacher/Student Love," *Educational Theory* 55, no. 1 (2005): 79–95.

Where this book is distributed in the UK, Europe and the rest of the world, this is by Palgrave Macmillan, a division of Macmillan Publishers Limited, registered in England, company number 785998, of Houndmills, Basingstoke, Hampshire RG21 6XS.

Palgrave Macmillan is the global academic imprint of the above companies and has companies and representatives throughout the world.

Palgrave® and Macmillan® are registered trademarks in the United States, the United Kingdom, Europe and other countries.

ISBN-13: 978-0-230-60608-1
ISBN-10: 0-230-60608-3

Library of Congress Cataloging-in-Publication Data

Cho, K. Daniel.
    Psychopedagogy : Freud, Lacan, and the psychoanalytic theory of
    education/K. Daniel Cho.
        p. cm. — (Education, psychoanalysis, social transformation)
    Includes bibliographical references and index.
    ISBN 0-230-60608-3
    1. Psychoanalysis and education. 2. Freud, Sigmund, 1856–1939. 3. Lacan,
Jacques, 1901–1981. I. Title.

LB1092.C56 2009
370.15—dc22   2008054868

A catalogue record of the book is available from the British Library.

Design by Macmillan Publishing Solutions.

First edition: May 2009

10 9 8 7 6 5 4 3 2 1

Printed in the United States of America.

For my parents, Seihwan and Jei-Jin Cho

Contents

List of Figures

Acknowledgments

My understanding of psychoanalysis owes itself to Kenneth Reinhard. Ken taught me to see Lacan as a closer reader of Freud—an approach that informs every aspect of this book. He is responsible for my attending the inaugural Seminar in Experimental Critical Theory at the University of California Humanities Research Institute in Irvine, California, in 2004, where I learned from renowned scholars working in the field of psychoanalysis. And Ken's Mellon-Sawyer seminar on "The Ethics of the Neighbor" gave me an invaluable education. His intellectual prowess and personal generosity still serve as a model for me. Of course, any shortcomings of this book are my responsibility alone. I am also greatly indebted to Douglas Kellner. Doug's supervision and encouragement supported me while I was toying with these ideas in my dissertation work. His knowledge of European intellectual history is bottomless, from which I frequently drew in many conversations over the years. His guidance remains indispensable to me, even today. A generous dissertation fellowship from the Hayman Endowment of the Semel Institute for Neuroscience and Human Behavior at UCLA funded the writing of the dissertation in which many of these ideas first appeared. This book literally could not have been possible without the enthusiasm and support of jan jagodzinski and Mark Bracher. It is my great fortune to know these two giants. And it is a great honor that my book appears in their series. I want to thank Fredric Jameson and Alenka Zupancic for reading early versions of some of the chapters. On a more personal note, I want to thank friends at two institutions for stimulating conversations over the years. At UCLA, Tyson Lewis, Richard Kahn, Clayton Pierce, Dolores Calderon,

Miguel Zavala, Tammy Shel, and Richard van Heertum. At Otterbein College, Debbie Halbert, Paul Eisenstein, Margaret Koehler, Karen Steigman, Phyllis Burns, Eric Jones, Wendy Sherman-Heckler, and Leslie Ortquist-Ahrens. Finally, I especially want to thank my family who supported me throughout the years. To my wife, Haelyn, my sons, Jameson and Henry, my brother Brian and his wife Sophia, and above all, my parents, Seihwan and Jei-Jin, to whom this book is dedicated: thank you for endowing me with strength, energy, joy, and faith.

Early versions of chapters 4, 7, and 8 appeared in the following journals under these titles: "*Wo es war*: Psychoanalysis, Marxism, and Subjectivity," *Educational Philosophy and Theory* 39, no. 7 (2007): 703–719; "Teaching Abjection: A Response to the War on Terror," *Teaching Education* 16, no. 2 (2005): 103–115; and "Lessons of Love: Psychoanalysis and Teacher/Student Love," *Educational Theory* 55, no. 1 (2005): 79–95.

Introduction: Pedagogy *with* Psychoanalysis

Jacques Lacan's approach to psychoanalysis is more than a clinical model; it is a robust interpretative framework as well. Its infusion into such disciplines as philosophy, literature, film and cultural studies, religious studies, and political science—to name only a few—has yielded not only some of the most fascinating insights but also a radical rethinking of the very stakes on which those fields stand. It has done so because psychoanalysis goes beyond the surface to uncover the libidinal investments made in the ongoing projects in those fields. And because of the insight it affords into the literary, the textual, and the human, Lacanian psychoanalysis has become a sine qua non in the theoretical humanities.

Psychoanalysis's infusion into the theoretical humanities is unsurprising since Sigmund Freud, throughout his oeuvre, revealed an abiding interest in literature, art, politics, society, religion, and such matters. But of the potential disciplinary fields to which psychoanalysis can make a contribution, Freud singles out one: "None of the applications of psycho-analysis has excited so much interest and aroused so many hopes, and none, consequently, has attracted so many capable workers, as its use in the theory and practice of education."[1] Yet, he goes on to say that while recognizing "the *bon mot* which lays it down that there are three impossible professions—educating, healing and governing,"[2] he regrets that most of his life's work was "fully occupied with the second of them," at the exclusion of education. "But," Freud interjects, "this does not mean that I overlook the high social value of the work done by those . . . who are engaged in education."[3]

Later, Freud very briefly revisits the subject of education in his *New Introductory Lectures on Psycho-Analysis,* telling his audience: "There is one topic which I cannot pass over so easily—not, however, because I understand particularly much about it or have contributed very much to it."[4] "I must mention it," he continues, "because it is so exceedingly important, so rich in hopes for the future, perhaps the most important of all the activities of analysis." After suggesting that his daughter's work on education somehow compensates for his lack of attention to it,[5] "the most important of all the activities of analysis," Freud tries his hand at marking out the contours of what a psychoanalytic inquiry into education might entail. For Freud, the primary task of education is to teach the child "to control his instincts,"[6] that is, education must "inhibit, forbid and suppress," but since "this suppression of instincts involves the risk of neurotic illness," "the only appropriate preparation for the profession of education is a thorough psycho-analytic training."[7] For Freud, education is the process of learning to curb the drives, and psychoanalysis is the theory that can aid in understanding that process.

If there is something profoundly dissatisfying in Freud's attempt to think of "the application of psycho-analysis to education,"[8] perhaps it is because he sees psychoanalysis's relationship to education on the order of its relationship to the humanistic disciplines: that is, psychoanalysis and education are distinctive fields that can later be brought together. In this way, the relevance of psychoanalysis in education is reduced to that of *application*: psychoanalytic education is merely an education to which psychoanalysis is applied. Yet, if the "bon mot" that ties psychoanalysis, education, and politics together as "the impossible professions" has any meaning at all, then surely it must be that all three fields are *not* completely distinct but are somehow inextricably linked so that one cannot be evoked without already evoking the other two. Education—if the bon mot holds true—therefore should be thought as possessing a more intimate relation with psychoanalysis than the theoretical humanities: if the theoretical humanities invite the intervention of psychoanalysis, then education cannot do without it.

The present book probes at the sites where the association as "impossible professions" breaks down the imagined wall
separating psychoanalysis and education. At these sites psychoanalysis is already pedagogy, and pedagogy is already psychoanalysis. The wager is that something more interesting than
Freud's "curb your enthusiasm" is to be found.[9] It is called
"psychopedagogy" in order to convey that at stake is not the
application of psychoanalysis to pedagogy but, much rather, the
ways in which psychoanalysis and pedagogy are intertwined,
coterminous. Psychoanalysis cannot be applied to pedagogy,
because pedagogy is already found *within* it. That is to say,
psychoanalysis utilizes and depends upon pedagogy in order to
formulate its theory and concepts.[10] Accordingly, the analyst-
analysand relationship is envisaged as a special type of pedagogical relationship in which the latter learns what is stored in
the unconscious. More than rhetoric, these pedagogical motifs
represent a theory of education and pedagogy in their own right.
At the heart of *psychopedagogy* is thus an attempt to elucidate
this theory already embedded within psychoanalysis by focusing
on these pedagogical motifs.

The specific interpretation of psychoanalysis under examination here is Jacques Lacan's momentous "return to Freud."
Lacan's theoretical contributions to the history of psychoanalytic
thought are among the most original and most important, but
they also have a reputation for being among the most challenging. Some of this challenge has to do with Lacan's idiosyncratic
style of discourse.[11] Most, however, has to do with the fact that
Lacan's thought develops over time, and he never wrote a mag-
num opus that contained the summation of his views. Instead,
we are left with the transcripts of Lacan's famous seminars,
which were conducted between the 1950s and 1970s, to witness
the dynamism of his thought firsthand. In terms of writing,
Lacan only left a volume's worth of essays, the *Écrits*.[12] All of
this leaves his thought in fragmentary form, utterly untotaliz-
able. Trying to fabricate a synthesis out of Lacan's fragments
can be a frustrating, even impossible, task. Obtaining even the
slightest handle on Lacan's thought requires combing over the

transcripts of his seminars (many of which are yet to appear in print and even fewer have been translated into English, posing further difficulties) and correlating those ideas with his various *écrits*—as one could imagine, this work demands the highest amount of patience. Effective construction of psychopedagogy will therefore require some explication of Lacan's thought, and that thought will be approached here as deriving from a close reading of Freud. It is always helpful to remember that historically Lacan came to prominence out of a critique of the so-called ego-psychologists, Heinz Hartmann, Ernst Kris, and Rudolph Lowenstein. Against ego-psychology's attempt to lower psychoanalysis to the level of a mere psychology by reducing Freud's thought to the ego-superego-id complex, Lacan, through a close reading of Freud's texts, emphasized the importance Freud placed on such fundamental concepts as the unconscious, the drive or instinct, repetition, and transference. For Lacan, psychoanalysis was officially inaugurated by Freud's revolutionary discovery of the unconscious; its framework was built on the concepts of the drive, sexuality, repetition, and transference, and it was capped with a critical understanding of the ego's function. Therefore anything that does not acknowledge the whole of Freud's thought, especially what Lacan calls "the four fundamental concepts" of, the unconscious, the drive or instinct, repetition, and transference, cannot go by the name psychoanalysis. For these reasons, Lacan will always be discussed here within his proper Freudian context, even reaching as far back as Freud's earliest, so-called prepsychoanalytic, writings in order to give a panoramic view of the development of Lacan's thought. The picture of psychopedagogy that will emerge as a result is that of a pedagogical thought that is already present and at work in Freud—archived, as it were, in his original texts—and is rediscovered by Lacan's close reading.

This book is organized into two parts. Part I, "Prolegomena to Any Future Psychopedagogy," does not so much give an exhaustive account of psychopedagogy as it does mark out its basic contours—hence, a prolegomena. It comprises three chapters, each focused on the pedagogical idea through which a key psychoanalytic concept is formulated: the unconscious, resistance, and transference, respectively. These chapters are intended to be read in order. Read this way, "Prolegomena" presents the development of the larger theory of pedagogy—what is being called psychopedagogy—as follows. In Chapter 1, psychoanalysis is seen as a particular kind of learning, one that is interested in not just any kind of knowledge but rather knowledge that is specifically traumatic. However, traumatic knowledge does not come in generic form; rather, it is always unconscious. Thus Chapter 1 is devoted to explicating the psychoanalytic concept of the unconscious: the major contention is that the Freudian unconscious is always ideational in content, never emotional, which Lacan makes clear by describing it as a discourse. But if traumatic knowledge is unconscious, then Freud and Lacan contend that one, paradoxically, already knows it, for the unconscious is ever present. Thus learning the unconscious is always a matter of *re*learning it. The unconscious is unconscious because the knowledge contained within was first experienced with a certain amount of reproach or pain. It follows that relearning the unconscious will be always met with a certain amount of resistance on the learner's part. The nature and kind of these resistances are taken up in Chapter 2. Chapter 3 argues that psychoanalytic pedagogy is not interested in didactically disseminating the knowledge of the unconscious but rather in helping the analysand overcome or work through the resistances that prevent the unconscious from being heard. The strongest tool for this working-through is the transference.

Part II, "Secondary Revisions," is composed of a series of studies that draw and expand upon ideas developed in "Prolegomena" by deploying them within the context of the more narrowly defined conception of education as formal schooling. "Secondary revision" is the name Freud gives to the process in which the disparate contents of dreams are reelaborated as a coherent narrative.[13] Like their namesake, these chapters yield more condensed pictures of what psychopedagogy indeed is by rearticulating the "Prolegomena" within the context of a more localized theoretical study. Each chapter, in a way, uses the findings of Part I as the optic for analyzing and criticizing a particular issue or topic in educational studies. Examined are a wide variety of issues, such as critical pedagogy, love, politics, and the rhetoric of the academic and standardization. As such, these chapters demonstrate the various productivities of psychopedagogy. As these chapters are topical rather than systematic, they can be read in any order.

It should be said that the present book makes no claims on being the definitive word on a general Lacanian psychoanalytic theory of pedagogy. This "Prolegomena" and "Secondary Revisions" are neither exhaustive nor definitive. Rather, they more modestly claim to have identified only certain fundamental concepts thus laying down a solid groundwork on which a larger theoretical edifice can be built. The hope is that the present book will inspire others to articulate what they see a Lacanian theory of pedagogy entailing, to make further connections in the Freudian field.

Finally, it is especially apropos of the current project, *psychopedagogy,* that Lacan always understood his intervention in the training of analysts. His mandate to the next generation of psychoanalysts was to know their Freud, an intervention that was performed in the context of the seminar no less. Another way of understanding Lacan's contribution to the history of psychoanalysis would be to say that his intervention was more pedagogical than academic. I already mentioned the way Lacanian psychoanalysis has become a fixture in the theoretical humanities; given the pedagogical nature of his intervention and discourse, it is high time that Lacanian psychoanalysis became a fixture in educational studies.[14]

Part I

Prolegomena to Any Future Psychopedagogy

The Unconscious: A Form of Knowledge

Sigmund Freud was a terrible hypnotist. And this we know not from hearsay but by Freud's own admission. Thinking back to the time before psychoanalysis came into being, to the time when he was still training at Hippolyte Bernheim's clinic in Nancy, France, Freud recalls feeling that such a thing as an "art" of hypnosis "really did exist . . . as if it could be learnt from Berhheim."[1] "But," he confesses, "as soon as I tried to practice it on my own patients, I noticed that *my* powers at least were severely restricted in this respect and that, if I could not make a patient somnambulistic in the first three attempts, I had no means of doing so at all" ("Studies," 111, original emphasis). Freud even gives a quite comical account of his troubles:

> I soon tired of giving the reassuring command, "You are going to sleep. Sleep!" and hearing the objection whenever the degree of hypnosis was slight, "But Doctor, I'm not sleeping at all," only then to have to propose the all too delicate distinction, "Of course I don't mean normal sleep, I mean hypnosis. You see, you're hypnotized, you can't open your eyes etc. In any case I don't need you to sleep, and so on." (111–12)

And yet, Freud, at this early stage, still regarded himself as a practitioner of a specific school of psychotherapy that held hypnosis as an integral technique. What was Freud to do? "I was presented with a choice," he tells us, "either I could refrain from practising the cathartic method in most of the cases which might have been suited to it, or I could experiment by using the method without somnambulism in those cases where the degree of hypnotic influence was slight or even doubtful" (111). Freud is at a crossroads; he must make an important decision: either continue on in a practice not suited to his talents or go his own way. He decides the latter, proceeding without the tool of hypnosis. Freud's decision is groundbreaking as it represents a break with the school of therapy he was trained in and his first step toward psychoanalysis.

Meanwhile, the decision to abandon hypnosis has serious implications for Freud's practice:

> In doing without somnambulism, it was possible that I was depriving myself of a precondition without which the cathartic method seemed impracticable. The basis of the method was, of course, that in an altered state of consciousness patients could access memories and recognize connections of a kind which they claimed were not present in their normal state of consciousness. (112)

The illness is first caused by some kind of trauma.[2] But the memory of that original traumatic event is missing from consciousness, lying somewhere beyond its purview. The (prepsychoanalytic) cathartic method revolves around the ability to access this missing memory, access afforded by hypnosis. As hypnosis is a method Freud decides to no longer practice, he is bereft of the practical technique for accessing the key to curing his patient's neuroses.

However, Freud accepts the premise of the school he is trained in, namely, that the key lies in accessing this, call it, supraconscious memory. But without hypnosis, he is unable to follow through in practice. Then, he remembers something from his Bernheim days: a demonstration. A woman, in a state of hypnosis, is told by Bernheim that he is invisible to her, and when asked, upon awakening, whether she remembers seeing Bernheim, she swears she does not. "But," Freud recounts, "he would not let it go at that"; Bernheim continued the demonstration by putting "his hand on her forehead so that she would think back and, lo and behold, she did finally relate everything that she claimed not to have perceived in her somnambulistic state and not to have been cognizant of in her waking state" (113). What in this demonstration strikes Freud is the specific way Bernheim uses hypnosis. In Freud's training, hypnosis is used, as a rule, to expand the patient's consciousness to encompass the traumatic supraconscious memory. However, in this demonstration, Bernheim uses hypnosis to make the woman *forget* something, namely, that she has seen him. To make her remember, he simply places his hands on her forehead, which, to be sure, is a nonhypnotic technique. Freud hypothesizes that the limits of consciousness can be extended *without* the aid of hypnosis. Freud is therefore convinced that his patient's lost memories are "only seemingly forgotten when the patient is awake and can be called forth again by a gentle summons" (112): a touch of the hand on the forehead.

Freud takes Bernheim's demonstration as a model for an experimental procedure. Instead of using hypnosis to facilitate the cathartic process, Freud would simply place his hands on his patients' foreheads and instruct them that the memories would return to consciousnesses simply under the pressure of his hands. The experimental technique worked remarkably well, even beyond Freud's expectations, as his patients were able to recall much of what was previously regarded as forgotten. What becomes apparent to Freud is that when a patient is unable to remember the crucial events of the original trauma, it does not reflect a feeble or limited consciousness but, rather, an overactive critical faculty. That is to say, the patient indeed knows the information in question either in part or in whole but is prevented from remembering it. Freud writes:

> Eventually I became so bold that when patients answered "I can't see anything" or "Nothing came to mind," I would explain to them that this was an impossibility, that they were sure to have discovered the right thing, it was just that they didn't think that they had, and had dismissed it. . . . And I was, in fact, right

every time: the patients had not yet learnt to relax their critical faculty, had dismissed the emerging memory or idea because they thought it was of no use, just something that had come up, a disruption, and after they had told me about it, it proved to be the right one every time. (113–14)

In Freud's view, the main obstacle to remembering is not consciousness's narrow threshold but this, what he calls, critical faculty. At this early and, to be sure, highly experimental stage, Freud suggests that analysts cope with the critical faculty by teaching their patients to relax it. However, as psychoanalysis comes into its own, Freud revises this position: the critical faculty—or, resistances—must be confronted and overcome rather than simply relaxed. The move from relaxing to overcoming in Freud's theory will be taken up in Chapter 3. Here, it is enough to say that even at this early, highly provisional, iteration of psychotherapeutic theory (it cannot yet be called "psychoanalysis"), remembering is presented as a skill that can be learned through the analytic process itself thus making recourse to hypnosis unnecessary. Another way of saying it is that Freud rejects hypnosis in favor of pedagogy. In fact, Freud feels so strongly in the pedagogical potential of analytic work that as he continues working with neurotics he even eschews his own Bernheim-inspired technique.

II

The change Freud makes in technique may appear minor, but the theoretical implications are legion, as demonstrated by the move from hypnosis to pedagogy. Indeed, it leads to nothing short of the discovery of psychoanalysis itself. In supposing that the patient *needs* hypnosis to expand the realm of consciousness, the Bernheim school of psychotherapy understands the inability to recall the traumatic past as the result of a sievelike memory. Some memories are retained by consciousness, others are not. It is not that the individual subject wants to forget, but that trauma is especially difficult to keep within consciousness. The individual is understood here as having a passive role.

Because he finds so much success with his quasi–Bernheimian technique, even to the point of making that technique itself obsolete, Freud comes to a different conclusion: "What seemed to me perhaps stranger still was that numbers and dates which were apparently long forgotten could be recovered by means of a similar procedure, so proving that memory is more accurate than one would expect" (114). Freud further unpacks the theoretical implications in the paper "On the Psychotherapy of Hysteria," the reflective conclusion to the dossier *Studies in Hysteria*. With the help of the cases collected in *Studies*, Freud ascertains the common thread to all the missing memories: "They were all of a distressing nature, fit to arouse the affects of shame, self-reproach, psychical pain and the feeling of impairment" (270). The events that are missing from consciousness are, according to Freud, not simply difficult; rather, they cause injury to the individual.[3] Trauma, for Freud, describes neither the nature of the event itself nor the content of its memorialization; it describes the effect of the event on the individual. Distress, shame, self-reproach, pain, impairment—these words all describe the type of impact that can turn an ordinary event into a full-blown trauma. While the vast majority of people would agree that the Holocaust, for example, is horrible and difficult to understand, not everyone experiences it as a trauma. The Holocaust becomes traumatic when it causes the individual pain by making the individual bear some sort of psychic stress or injury such as shame or guilt. Whereas *difficulty* is in some sense experienced objectively, *trauma* is experienced subjectively or existentially. The difference between difficulty and trauma is why many people can talk "factually" about the Holocaust while still more can regurgitate facts and figures on exams without a sense of shame or injury. In defining trauma relationally, Freud reveals the *incentive* for forgetting traumatic events: traumas are supraconscious not because they are in themselves horrible events, though they certainly might be, but rather because of the negative affects they stir up in the individual. The individual, for

Freud, has an active hand in forgetting. Indeed, the individual commits an *act* of forgetting and usually for good reason. And without this dimension of injury or wounding, an event, while difficult, raises no problems for the conscious memory.

As the individual is, for Freud, figured as an active agent in the process of forgetting memories, the memory is not sieve-like. Traumatic memories never simply slip through consciousness. Consciousness stores them but in a way that does not interfere with its operation. How then are they stored? The answer leads to the very theoretical innovation on which Freud builds psychoanalysis, namely, the unconscious. The unconscious is a paradox: it is the part of consciousness that is no longer conscious. Not supraconscious but literally not-conscious (*Unbewusste*). To get a better handle on this paradox, it is perhaps better to describe the unconscious as the reverse or underside of consciousness itself.[4] And this is why hypnosis is unnecessary: since the unconscious is not external to consciousness, not outside of its purview, but its exact other side, no amount of expanding consciousness leads to it. But neither does this mean that the unconscious remains inaccessible. It only means that access to the unconscious must be fought out *within* consciousness itself. Consciousness, as it were, must pass through *itself* or, to put it another way, it must cross its own inner split. This paradoxical location means that the unconscious is indeed a particular kind of conscious knowledge: it is the form taken by traumatic knowledge.

What Freud gains from all of his early clinical experience is a whole new theoretical premise for practical work. "I decided," Freud recounts, "to work on the assumption that my patients knew everything that was of any pathogenic significance and that it was simply a question of making them communicate this" (113). Freud's new premise turns everything in Bernheim around. The memory is not porous; rather, it is sound, indeed too sound. The individual is not ignorant or feebleminded but knowledgeable and capable. The individual is also not passive but active. The knowledge itself—that is, everything of "pathogenic significance"—is not supraconscious; it is unconscious.

Trauma is not forgotten but *repressed*. The key to unlocking neurosis is not in expanding consciousness through hypnosis but in communicating what is in the unconscious through analytic work. The upshot of these reversals is psychoanalysis.

III

"The unconscious comprises," Freud writes in his paper "The Unconscious," "on the one hand, acts which are merely latent, temporarily unconscious, but which differ in no respect from conscious ones, and, on the other hand, processes such as repressed ones, which if they were to become conscious would be bound to stand out in the crudest contrast to the rest of the conscious process."[5] Psychoanalysis is interested in the latter, that is, the repressed content of the unconscious.

According to popular speak, "repressed" usually refers to an emotion. On this popular definition, when someone is said to be repressed, what is usually meant is that the person has suppressed all emotional feelings. For example, a sexually repressed individual is said to be void of feelings of lust or desire. Nothing could be further from Freud's understanding of repression than this popular notion. In the introduction to *Studies in Hysteria*, Freud and Josef Breuer note that the difference between neurosis and illness is that the latter is the result of a physical injury whereas the former is the result of a psychical trauma, which is signaled by the "affect of fright" (*Studies*, 9). "Any experience," they write, "which gives rise to the distressing affects of fright, anxiety, shame or psychical pain can have this effect and, understandably, it depends on the sensitivity of the person concerned . . . whether the experience will take on traumatic value." Even at this early stage in Freud's thought, the vast distance separating his position and the popular understanding of repression is evident. Neurotics, for Freud, are not people who have suppressed their feelings and emotions; rather, they are people who are overwhelmed by affect: trauma elicits overwhelmingly intense feelings of fear, shame, and anxiety, culminating in a neurosis.

Freud provides a clear example in the case history of Miss Lucy R., one of his earliest patients. Miss Lucy R., who is employed as a governess, comes to Freud, tormented by the smell of burnt pudding. Through the course of analysis, Freud suggests to his patient that she secretly loves her employer. Miss Lucy R., perhaps surprisingly, does not dispute Freud's suggestion at all. Quite the contrary, she readily admits it, even going so far as to confess that she had once hoped to marry him. According to the popular understanding of repression as the suppression of affect, Miss Lucy R. should have contradicted Freud as all amorous feelings should have been suppressed. The popular notion of repression leads to a dead end. However, Freud probes further. During one session, Miss Lucy R. notifies Freud that the smell of burnt pudding has dissipated, but now she is tormented by the smell of cigar smoke. Through a series of questions, Miss Lucy R. recalls a memory: her employer and his bookkeeper, who is also a family friend, are sharing a cigar; once finished, the bookkeeper says goodbye to her employer's children by kissing them on the lips; having witnessed this, her employer flies into a rage. Witnessing her employer chastise a family friend bothers her, since if he treats a friend that way, then she can only imagine what he would do to a mere employee like her. Freud pursues the matter still further, at which point Miss Lucy R. remembers another scene. This time a lady friend says goodbye to the children by kissing them. Again, her employer is enraged and tells her that if it happens again, she would be fired. "This scene," as Freud puts it, "crushed her hopes." "If he can set on me and threaten me like that over something so slight," Miss Lucy R. tells Freud, "then I have made a mistake. He can't ever have had any warm feelings for me" (121). In Freud's assessment, being rebuked by her employer—a man for whom she had fond feelings—shames Miss Lucy R. to such an extent that she repressed the memory of the event. What she represses however is not love but the memory scene.

Returning to Freud and Breuer, they write: "We are bound to assert that the psychical trauma, or more precisely, the memory of it, operates like a foreign body which must still be regarded as a present and effective agent" (10). What they are suggesting is that the repressed is not the traumatic event itself but its memory. Or, to put it another way, repressed is any and all *knowledge* of the traumatic event. In the case of Miss Lucy R., what is repressed is the memory, knowledge, or, as Freud has it, the *scene*, of her beloved employer's violent rage over seeing his children kissed on the lips. At seeing this rage, a conflict arises in her between the knowledge that he blatantly disregards her and the fondness she has for him. The conflict is resolved by splitting these two parts: the knowledge on the one hand and the emotion on the other. The scene as well as any associated knowledge is repressed, made unconscious. The emotion, however, remains and becomes attached to the smell of cigar smoke and burnt pudding, giving those scents an additional libidinal charge. Once Miss Lucy R. remembers this scene, she is able, as Freud and Breuer have it, to put "words to the affect" (10); and her situation, as a result, changes dramatically, her sense of smell returning.

As Freud's thought continues to develop—above all, with the landmark *Papers on Metapsychology*—the ideational, as opposed to emotional, character of the unconscious becomes better defined. In the first *Paper*, "Instincts and Their Vicissitudes," Freud claims this of an instinct:

> If now we apply ourselves to considering mental life from a *biological* point of view, an "instinct" appears to us as a concept on the frontier between the mental and the somatic, as the psychical representative of the stimuli originating from within the organism and reaching the mind, as a measure of the demand made upon the mind for work in consequence of its connection with the body. (*SE* 14:121–22, original emphasis)

This single sentence contains a manifold of important information, but what concerns us here is Freud's suggestion that what is referred to as a singular entity, the instinct, is in actuality a composite of the instinct itself and its psychical representative or *representative idea*.

Repression—that is, the action of "turning something away, and keeping it at a distance, from the conscious" (*SE* 14:147)—impacts only the "psychical (ideational) representative of the instinct" (148), and not the instinct itself. This is because the "instinct," as Freud understands it, "can never become an object of consciousness—only the idea that represents the instinct can" (177). Freud's claim is, in essence, that individuals repress ideas that represent the instinct to consciousness. What Freud, in the earlier *Studies*, described as a *scene* is now being described as a *psychical* or *ideational representative*. Nothing could be further from the emotions than Freud's language of representation.

Freud so emphatically believes repression is always the repression of ideational content that in "The Unconscious," he writes: "It is surely of the essence of an emotion that we should be aware of it, i.e. that it should become known to consciousness. Thus the possibility of the attribute of unconsciousness would be completely excluded as far as emotions, feelings and affects are concerned" (177). Freud could not be clearer that repression does not refer to the suppression of emotion. For the purpose of clarity, Freud's notion of the ideational representative will be referred to simply as knowledge: thus what remains repressed in the unconscious is always some sort of traumatic knowledge. In this way, psychoanalysis can be understood as a kind of learning process: the process of learning traumatic knowledge.

However, one should be careful not to understand Freud as neglecting affect, for he indeed has a theory of the emotions. When repression occurs—that is, when some traumatic knowledge is made not-conscious—it is loosened from an accompanying "quota of affect" (152). This newly freed affect can then become attached to other ideas, dissipate, heighten into anxiety, or remain free-floating. In its separated state, the emotion is usually misrecognized as something other than the traumatic knowledge's emotional concomitant. Once the traumatic knowledge is learned from the unconscious, this free-radical affect becomes thrown into new and proper light. An example would be Freud's patient known as the Ratman. While in the army, the Ratman has a conversation with one of his commanding officers—"a captain with a Czech name."[6] In this conversation, the captain recounts a form of torture involving the use of rats. Hearing the Czech captain describe this rat-torture makes the man sick. When the sickness escalates into a full-blown case of obsessive compulsion, he comes to see Freud. Through the course of analysis, Freud determines that the Ratman has repressed the traumatic knowledge of having fiercely attacked his father in childhood (the trauma here being the feeling of guilt for having attacked his father). Once repressed, this knowledge becomes separated from its affective component—namely, his hatred for his father—and the lingering affect is displaced onto the person of the Czech captain. The Ratman's hatred, which, to be sure, was never unconscious or repressed but only displaced, is nevertheless misrecognized by him as everything but what it actually is. He sees it as a sign that his captain is contemptibly sadistic, that he himself is a coward, even that women in general are repugnant. What he does not see it as is the companion to the traumatic knowledge that he hates his father.

IV

When Freud uses the phrase "ideational representative"—described here as traumatic knowledge—to designate the content of the unconscious, he is using a phrase that is original to him. This phrase, which is translated in English as "ideational representative," is, in the original German, *Vorstellungsrepräsentanz*, which is the combination of two words: *Vorstellung* and *Repräsentanz*. The fact that Freud invents a composite word is not unusual for the German language. However, the word itself is peculiar: *Vorstellung* roughly translates as "representation," "idea," or "conception"; and *Repräsentanz* roughly translates as "representative," in the legal sense, such as, an ambassador or lawyer. *Vorstellungsrepräsentanz* thus roughly translates to the "representation of the representative." Freud, in using the language of representation, means to draw a sharp line of distinction between affects and concepts. Thus clarifying that repressed content is never emotional but always ideational is not a superficial gesture; it is, rather, embedded within Freud's discourse.

No one understood the stakes of Freud's highly original language better than Jacques Lacan. In the seventh of his famed seminars, *The Ethics of Psychoanalysis*, Lacan draws attention to Freud's phrase:

> The thought processes insofar as they regulate by means of the pleasure principle the investment of the *Vorstellungen*, and the structure in which the unconscious is organized, the structure in which the underlying unconscious mechanisms are flocculated. And it is this which makes the small curds of representation, that is to say, something which has the same structure as the signifier—a point on which I insist. That is not just *Vorstellung*, but as Freud writes later in the same article on the unconscious, *Vorstellungsrepräsentanz*; and he thus turns *Vorstellung* into an associative and combinatory element. In that way the world of *Vorstellung* is already organized according to the possibilities of the signifier as such.[7]

Of the many interesting things going on in this passage, most pertinent for the present discussion is the way Lacan underscores Freud's representational language by using the term "signifier" from structural linguistics. The point Lacan is making to his seminarians is that, in Freud, the unconscious is a mode of representation. That is to say, while objects exist in the real—that is, outside of language—we can only know them in and through language, through discourse, which is why Lacan claims that "the unconscious is a language" (*S* III:11).

Lacan continues his discussion of Freud's terminology in seminar XI, *The Four Fundamental Concepts of Psychoanalysis*. In the session entitled "Tuché and Automaton," Lacan takes the opportunity "to stress what Freud, when he speaks of the unconscious, designates as that which essentially determines it, the *Vorstellungsrepräsentanz*" (*S* XI:60). "This means not," he continues, "as it has been mistranslated, the representative representative, but that which takes the place of the representation" (60), that is, the "representative of the representation" (218). Vorstellungsrepräsentanz is not representative in the sense of being the most exemplary of representatives but rather something that represents representation, something that takes the place of representation. "That which takes the place of representation," Lacan claims, in conclusion, "is the *Trieb*" (60), the instinct.

With the help of Lacan, the full implications of Freud's special terminology are now within grasp. Recall that, for Freud, only the instinct's representative—which we retranslated as knowledge— can become an object of consciousness and never the instinct itself. Freud calls repression that affects the instinct's initial representative *primal repression*, that is, "a first phase of repression, which consists in the psychical (ideational) representative of the instinct being denied entrance into the conscious" (*SE* 14:148). What Freud once described as a scene is now being more formally termed *Vorstellungsrepräsentanz*. By connecting this term with the instinct, Lacan clarifies that upon exploring the unconscious one is not hitting the bedrock of the psyche but rather Vorstellungsrepräsentanz, that is, knowledge that represents something else, namely, the instinct. Vorstellungsrepräsentanz is, in other words, a signifier, and what it signifies is the instinct. To put it another way, Vorstellungsrepräsentanz designates the mode through which the instinct speaks. By claiming that repressed in the unconscious is Vorstellungsrepräsentanz, Lacan reads Freud as having in mind a linguistic model of the unconscious insofar as it signifies or speaks the instinct. That is to say, when the unconscious emits Vorstellungsrepräsentanz, it speaks its knowledge in the language of the instinct. And this is why Lacan claims "the unconscious is structured like a language" (*S* XI:149).

V

For Lacan, a signifier always resides at the center of the unconscious, a fragment of knowledge that represents nothing else but the instinct itself: "What is essential is that he should see, beyond this signification, to what signifier—to what irreducible, traumatic, non-meaning—he is, as a subject, subjected" (250–51). Lacan gives two examples of this repressed signifier. The first is taken from the work of his pupil Serge Leclaire. In one of his cases, Leclaire discovers the nonsensical signifier *Poordjeli* at the center of one of his patient's unconscious. The name of this patient is Philippe, and he is obsessed with unicorns, which, in French, is *licorne*. The Lacanian commentator, Eric Laurent, elaborates on the significance of Leclaire's discovery:

> Philippe had obsessions that could be traced to the fact that he was defined, not as a bad boy, but rather as "poor Philippe" (*pauvre Philippe*). His mother always referred to him as "poor Philippe" and the connection of the sound of "au" in "*pauvre*" and "o" in "*licorne*" was stressed by Leclaire, who showed that "*pauvre Philippe*" was the sound that put Philippe to bed [*lit*]. . . . Leclaire pointed out that Philippe could be defined in terms of a chain that could be written as follows: Poor (d) J'e-Li (Poordjeli) including "poor Philippe," the "je" (I) of the subject, and "li" from Philippe, *licorne*, and *lit* (bed).[8]

Lacan's second example is taken from Freud's patient known as the Wolfman. The pseudonym, Wolfman, is derived from the nature of his symptom: he is plagued by dreams of wolves. The Wolfman recounts his recurring dream to Freud thus:

> I dreamed that it is night and I am lying in my bed. . . . Suddenly the window opens of its own accord and terrified, I see that there are a number of white wolves sitting in the big walnut tree outside the window. There were six or seven of them. The wolves were white all over and looked more like foxes or sheepdogs because they had big tails like foxes and their ears were pricked up like dogs watching something. Obviously fearful that the wolves were going to gobble me up I screamed and woke up. (*Wolfman*, 227)

Through the course of treating the Wolfman, Freud comes to theorize something he calls the "primal scene" (236). The primal scene is the language through which the Wolfman's traumatic knowledge is registered and made unconscious. Freud remains undecided on the exact accuracy of the recollected primal scene. "These previously unconscious memories," he writes, "do not even have to be true; they may be true, but their truth is often distorted and interspersed with fantasized elements" (250). What is important is that they are "fantasy-formations, drawing their inspiration from riper years, intended as a symbolic representation, so to speak, of real wishes and interests" (248). Note that Freud calls the primal scene the "symbolic representation" of "real wishes and interests." Lacan seizes on the linguistic tone of Freud's description, presenting the primal scene as an exemplary case of the primary signifier.

The traumatic event is thus never obliterated from the mind but, rather, is stored as knowledge in the form of the primary signifier in the unconscious. Traumatic knowledge is knowledge translated into the language of the unconscious. Any other signifying material that can be associated with the primary signifier will "experience that same fate as what was primally repressed" (*SE* 14:148)—he calls this secondary repression, *repression proper*. Made up of the primally repressed primary signifier and the repressed associated content, "the unconscious," Lacan describes, "becomes a chain of signifiers,"[9] a language unto itself. Elsewhere, Lacan elaborates: "The unconscious is fundamentally structured, woven, *chained*, meshed, by language. And not only does the signifier play as big a role there as the signified does, but it plays the fundamental role. In fact, what characterizes language is *the system of signifiers* as such" (*S* III:119, emphasis added).

Psychoanalysis is not a doctrine of nihilism: the claim that traumatic knowledge is stored in the unconscious in no way suggests that it can never be accessed. If anything, the problem psychoanalysis presents is the exact opposite. The linguistic nature of the unconscious means traumatic knowledge *can* be spoken—indeed, the unconscious, as Lacan puts it, is "knowledge that speaks all by itself" (*S* XVII:70). Though not impossible, speaking the unconscious is not straightforward either; doing so involves a tremendous amount of work. Freud likens this work to that of translation—thus underlining the linguistic nature of the unconscious:

How are we to arrive at a knowledge of the unconscious? It is of course only as something conscious that we know it, after it has

> undergone transformation or translation into something con-
> scious. Psycho-analytic work shows us every day that translation
> of this kind is possible. (*SE* 14:166)

Indeed, the entire dynamic of analytic work turns on the struggle
to speak forth repressed traumatic knowledge. Lacan however
cautions: "Interpretation is not open to any meaning" (*S* XI:250).
What this means is that the aim of psychoanalysis is strictly to
enable the unconscious to speak its traumatic knowledge, not to
impose or add meaning to it through, say, interpretation. The
reason Lacan cautions against interpreting the primary signifier
is that the primary signifier, "insofar as the primary signifier is
pure non-sense," is "not open to all meanings, but abolish[es]
them all" (252). Rather than unlocking some deep mysterious
meaning behind the primary signifier—after all, the primary
signifier always represents the instinct itself, which can never
become conscious as such—the goal of psychoanalysis is to take
responsibility for it, in all its traumatic fullness.

The wonderful Christopher Nolan film *Memento*[10] perfectly
demonstrates these psychoanalytic principles. The principal
character of this film is Leonard—a man who suffers short-
term memory loss from a head injury he suffers while trying to
stop his wife's murder. Leonard's motivation is to find his wife's
murderer and avenge his loss. Suffering from amnesia, Leonard
can only visualize fragmented scenes of his wife's murder. So,
to compensate for his lack of memory, Leonard uses an instant
camera to take photographs that he hopes will act as a prosthetic
memory. Piecing the photographs together, Leonard is led to a
man named Teddy. Leonard is convinced Teddy is his man, but
before he enacts his vengeance, Teddy reveals that Leonard's
wife was killed by none other than Leonard himself. Leonard,
as it happens, injected his wife, a diabetic, with a lethal amount
of insulin. The reason Leonard suffers short-term memory loss
has nothing to do with trying to stop a would-be killer—indeed,
there is no attack, in the first place. Rather, it is because he has
repressed the traumatic knowledge that he is his wife's killer. As
for the instant photographs, if read within their proper context,

they too would reveal the truth that Teddy is not the man who Leonard is looking for. But Leonard has misrecognized what the photos are in fact telling him. In other words, these photographs have undergone what Freud calls repression proper.

The obvious psychoanalytic concept at work here is repression insofar as Leonard represses the traumatic knowledge that he is his wife's murderer and all the associated photographs. However, Nolan's use of the visual medium of film attends to all the nuances of psychoanalytic thought. The unconscious is not represented as some complex of self-hate. Rather, it is visualized as a flash-back scene, which appears in the form of fragments that must be pieced together. This scene, which in the film is soundless, is separated from the associated affects of guilt and shame—affects that are displaced onto Teddy. But the true genius of the film is the use of the instant photographs. These photographs, if prop-erly recognized, would form a *signifying chain* leading ultimately to the original traumatic scene in which Leonard sees himself killing his wife. The unconscious, as it were, speaks its knowledge through the medium of these photos. As such, they must also be secondarily repressed, which Leonard accomplishes by misrec-ognizing the story they are telling. The original scene of killing his wife, which only comes to Leonard's memory in fragments, together with the chain of instant photographs, which he carries in his hand, is his unconscious. Leonard's "cure" would not be to take something meaningful from his wife's death. Rather, it would be to learn this traumatic knowledge in all its bare horror, and take responsibility for it as the truth of his being.

VI

The psychoanalytic stance may seem uncompromisingly severe. With the unconscious, psychoanalysis suggests that we indeed know more than we want to admit. Learning the unconscious is in fact an act of relearning. Slavoj Zizek dramatizes the severity of the psychoanalytic stance in the title of his book *For They Know Not What They Do*. The title of Zizek's book is a reference to Christ's well-known request that God forgive those responsible for his crucifixion since they "know not what they do." For Zizek, Christianity is therefore too lenient, since it accepts the sinner's ignorance regarding the sinfulness of their action at face value. "Psychoanalysis," Zizek explains, "is much more severe than Christianity: ignorance is *not* a sufficient reason for forgiveness since it conveys a hidden dimension of *enjoyment*."[11] The individual has a deep investment in "forgetting" traumatic knowledge, since that knowledge causes them injury. This incentive allows the individual to enjoy ignorance. This enjoyment to be had in remaining ignorant of traumatic knowledge is what Christianity, according to Zizek, totally misses. According to psychoanalysis, the unconscious means that one must be held responsible for traumatic knowledge. Psychoanalysis indicts where Christianity forgives. In refusing to forgive ignorance, psychoanalysis has an abiding interest in pedagogy, but it is also committed to a specific pedagogical aim: to teach the analysand to learn traumatic knowledge from the unconscious. It is an aim that is achieved only by allowing the unconscious to speak forth its signifiers.

2

On the Ego and Other Strategies of Resistance

I

The liberal political philosopher John Stuart Mill once wrote: "Men are not more zealous for truth than they often are for error."[1] What Mill means is that the truth is not easy to discover, and so rather than deal with the difficult work necessary to arrive at truth, people settle for the much easier goal of error. In writing this, Mill believes he is saying something deeply insightful, contentious, and even radical. But, for psychoanalysis, Mill's statement is a meaningless platitude.

Freud, as we saw, works with patients who are suffering from symptoms that are "the effects and remains of excitations that had influenced the nervous system as traumas."[2] If trauma is the "truth" of one's being, then one will of course be more zealous for "error," for who really wants to reexperience trauma? But Freud's analysis delves much further than Mill's: Freud maintains that traumatic knowledge only appears forgotten. In actuality, that knowledge is only unconscious. So what exactly is going on when his patients are unable to recall that knowledge? "What resulted from all of this," Freud writes in the postscript to *Studies in Hysteria*, "On the Psychotherapy of Hysteria," "as if of its own accord, was the thought of *defence*" (*Studies*, 270, original emphasis). On the premise that the missing knowledge is traumatic in nature—that is, it evokes "the kind of affect that one would like not to have experienced and would prefer to forget" (270)—the act of forgetting, Freud surmises, is not genuine ignorance but a defense against remembering. The logic is this: a traumatic event takes place, evoking negative feelings, such as shame or pain; and in order to put an end to those feelings, the event is repressed, but that repressed material often returns, stirring up the original traumatic pain. Naturally, the patient does not want such a thing to happen and, in the interest of self-protection, defends against the reentrance of repressed knowledge into consciousness. Thus the patient is unable to answer Freud's queries:

> The patient's self had been approached by an idea that proved to be intolerable, and aroused on the part of the self a force of repulsion, which had aimed to *defend* itself against this intolerable idea. This defence was in fact successful, the idea in question was forced out of consciousness and memory, and its psychical trace was, it seems, not to be found. (271)

The inability to remember is not a sign that the person is truly oblivious. Indeed, for Freud, the case is the exact opposite: the inability to remember is an act of *resistance* to a process that is forcing a painful confrontation with the traumatic truth. "The hysteric's not-knowing was, therefore," Freud concludes, "a more or less conscious not-wanting-to-know" (271). Clearly, Freud is far more radical than Mill: whereas Mill sees the zealousness for error as a sign of how difficult the truth is to find, Freud sees that zealousness as resistance to relearning the traumatic truth already in one's possession.

With the concept of resistance, Freud revises his earlier position that therapy depends on relaxing an overactive critical faculty. Such relaxing only offers temporary respite—if even that—and once outside the analytic context, all the untampered resistances are bound to return. Freud indeed eschews every method of mental relaxation—including even his Bernheim-inspired technique—and decides instead that the analyst's "task consists in overcoming this *resistance to association* through psychical work" (271, original emphasis). The emphasis on work is crucial. For Freud, psychoanalysis offers no easy way out: one must confront and overcome all the resistances to traumatic knowledge. To borrow a line from Karl Marx: "There is no royal road to science, and only those who do not dread the fatiguing climb of its steep paths have a chance of gaining its luminous summits."[3] The name Freud gives to this "fatiguing climb" is: working-through.

II

Grounded in the reality of the unconscious, psychoanalysis uncovers an unusual obstacle to the learning process. The trouble with learning traumatic knowledge is not that it is obscure or inscrutable. The trouble is that it is ubiquitous. For that reason, if learning does not take place, it is not because knowledge is hard to find but because the learner refuses this knowledge. The problem of psychoanalytic learning is thus the problem of resistance.

The unconscious is problematic to the individual not because it is too far but because it is too close. Lacan captures this troubling nearness with the dictum: "The unconscious is the discourse of the other."[4] In his seminar *The Ego in Freud's Theory and in the Technique of Psychoanalysis*, Lacan elaborates on this aspect of the unconscious through a discussion of the clinical context.[5] In the analytic situation, the analysand believes to be having a one-on-one conversation with the analyst. Analysis is, as far as the analysand is concerned, a conversation between one ego and another ego. Usually, such ego-to-ego conversation revolves around the analysand insisting that the analyst should act in the role of the expert and reveal all the secrets of the neurosis under question. However, "there is," Lacan cautions, "something outside this field which has every right to speak as *I*, and which makes this right manifest by coming into the world speaking as an *I*" (*S* II:8). The "something" to which Lacan alludes is, of course, the unconscious, which "completely eludes that circle of certainties by which man recognizes himself as ego." The unconscious thus emits signifiers, like some *other's discourse*—hence, "the unconscious is the discourse of the other"—rudely interrupting this ego-to-ego conversation, which is why Lacan, somewhat humorously, likens the unconscious to a "third party" (*S* II:52) who crashes a gathering where only two were invited. The unconscious, as described in the previous chapter, is "knowledge that speaks all by itself" (*S* XVII:70). Of course, the analyst knows full well that this unwanted "third party" is the rightful subject of analysis, but the analysand does not agree and vigorously resists its presence.

Take, as an example of the unconscious as third party, Freud's Ratman:

> In the next session he begins by saying that he must relate an actual incident from his childhood. After the age of 7, as he had already told me, he experienced a fear that his parents could guess his thoughts, a feeling that has persisted, actually, all his life. At the age of 12 he loved a little girl, the sister of a friend . . . but she was not as affectionate as he would have liked. And then the idea occurred to him that she would be loving towards him if misfortune befell him; the death of his father came involuntarily into his mind as one such possibility. He rejected this idea immediately and forcefully, and defends himself even now against the possibility that this might have been the expression of a "wish." It was simply "thought-association."[6]

The Ratman wants to tell Freud the story of failed love, but he ends up, somewhat inexplicably, revealing his wish for his father's death. The Ratman cannot understand why he would be saying anything of the sort since he believes there could be nothing more unlike him. So horrendous is the wish that the Ratman thinks it must not be he who speaks it but some foreign body who is using him as its mouthpiece. Someone else, not the Ratman, must be speaking, someone who the Ratman does not even recognize. The unconscious is of course this other that has entered the scene "involuntarily" and unannounced. The Ratman resists the unconscious by insisting he has misspoken. He has inadvertently made an erroneous "thought-association." Indeed, he has made a "thought-association," even a mistaken one, but one that speaks the truth nonetheless: "In analysis, truth emerges in the most clear-cut representative of the mistake" (*S* I:265).

III

Lacan diagrams the relations between the analyst, the analysand, and the unconscious as shown in Figure 2.1.

The positions on the diagram correspond to the different agents acting within the analytic context. What should be very clear from the outset is that, despite what the analysand thinks, there are not simply two but four entities present in analysis. In the lower left corner is the analysand's ego. In the upper right corner is the analyst's ego. In the lower right is the unconscious. And in the upper left is the position of the subject, a vacant position that the analysand struggles with the unconscious to occupy. The analysand, of course, wants to converse directly with the analyst's ego, represented here by vector aa'. Insofar as it represents talk that takes place between two egos, Lacan calls vector aa' the *imaginary relation* or *imaginary function*. Cutting across and disrupting the imaginary relation, like an uninvited third party, is the unconscious, which emerges as the discourse of the other to announce itself as subject (Es). It is necessary "to intervene in the system conditioned by the image of the ego," that is, the imaginary function, "so that an exchange" between the patient and the unconscious "can take place" (*S* II:52). The diagram captures this intervention with the intersection of the two vectors, which represents the dynamic struggle between the unconscious,

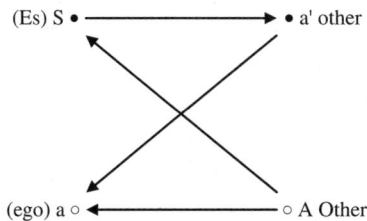

Figure 2.1   Lacan's diagram of the imaginary function of the ego and the discourse of the unconscious

breaking through the imaginary function with its signifiers, and the analysand, attempting to resist the unconscious by reconstituting the imaginary function:

> All this crystallization shows is the following, that the subject's discourse, in so far as it doesn't attain this full speech in which its base in the unconscious should be revealed, is already addressed to the analyst, is so made as to interest him, and is supported by this alienated form of being that one calls the *ego*. (*S* I:52, original emphasis)

Another way to read Lacan's diagram is to start from the position of the unconscious (A) and follow the arrows around the diagram. Read this way, the diagram suggests that the unconscious speaks to the patient in two ways. First, it speaks directly to the patient (vector Aa), which the patient, of course, resists. Analytic work involves forcing the patient to overcome these resistances so that the unconscious can be heard: "The analysis consists in getting him to become conscious of his relations, not with the ego of the analyst, but with all these Others who are his true interlocutors, whom he hasn't recognized" (*S* II:246). Thus the task of the analyst is not to engage with the patient as an ego, that is, as himself or herself. Rather, the analyst must serve as the mouthpiece of the unconscious. The analyst must speak the language of the unconscious—what Lacan refers to as "full speech" (*S* I:52) or "true speech" (*S* II:246). In other words, the unconscious, whose attempt at direct communication is met with resistance, is able to finally speak to the patient through the mouthpiece of the analyst (vector ASa'). "The analysis," Lacan thus finds, "must aim at the passage of true speech, joining the subject to an other subject, on the other side of the wall of language. That is the final relation of the subject to a genuine Other, to the Other who gives the answer one doesn't expect, which defines the terminal point of the analysis" (*S* II:246). This Other—the Other with a big O, the Other on the other side of the wall of imaginary talk, the Other with which the analyst arranges an encounter with the analysand—this Other is the Other of the unconscious.

IV

What are the strategies of resistance that are applied in the analytic setting to reconstruct the imaginary function against the irruptions of the unconscious? "In the first place," Freud begins his lecture on "Resistance and Repression," "then, when we undertake to restore a patient to health, to relieve him of the symptoms of his illness, he meets us with a violent and tenacious resistance, which persists throughout the whole length of the treatment."[7] One of the most famous cases of "violent and tenacious resistance" is Freud's patient Dora, of whom Freud writes: "Precisely that portion of the technical work which is the most difficult never came into question with this patient; for the factor of 'transference' . . . did not succeed in developing during the short treatment."[8] Freud gives us a brief window into Dora's problematic treatment: "When I told Dora that I would not avoid supposing that her affection for her father must at a very early moment have amounted to her being completely in love with him, she of course gave me her usual reply: 'I don't remember that'" (*Dora*, 49–50). After Dora directly rebuffs Freud, she changes the subject to apply Freud's interpretation to her cousin: "This little girl had . . . been the witness of a heated dispute between her parents, and, when Dora happened to come in on a visit soon afterwards, whispered in her ear: 'You can't think how I hate that person!' (pointing to her mother), 'and when she's dead I shall marry papa'" (50). "I am in the habit of regarding associations such as this," Freud writes, "which bring forward something that agrees with the content of an assertion of mine, as a confirmation from the unconscious of what I have said." Indeed: "No other kind of 'Yes' can be extracted from the unconscious; there is no such thing at all as an unconscious 'No.'"

Freud gives one more, almost humorous, account of Dora's difficult manner. The content of analytic work is a dream Dora has in which "a house was on fire" (56). "My father was standing beside my bed and woke me up. I dressed myself quickly. Mother wanted to stop and save her jewel-case; but Father said: 'I refuse to let myself and my two children be burnt for the sake of your jewel-case.'" Upon hearing Freud suggest that the jewel-case represents the female genitals, Dora retorts, "I knew you would say that" (61), which Freud takes as a resistance to the "knowledge that emerges from the repressed" (61, Note 11). Freud, however, continues his interpretation, giving Dora a quite lengthy explanation for the dream. Dora's response must have been succinct and negative because Freud only reports, "Naturally Dora would not follow me in this part of the interpretation" (62–63). To further illustrate his interpretation, Freud plants a book of matches on a stand where normally nothing is, and he asks her if she notices anything new. Of course, "she noticed nothing" (63). Freud goes on with his plan and asks her if she knows why children are forbidden from playing with matches. Dora's response: "Yes; on account of the risk of fire" (63). Her sarcasm is palpable, but Freud doggedly continues, hinting at something else, but she, again, plays dumb. Freud finally caves—"Very well, then"—and reveals the answer he had in mind—"The fear is that if they do they will wet their bed" (63). Again, Dora does not cooperate: "I know nothing about myself . . . but my brother used to wet his bed up till his sixth or seventh year; and it used sometimes to happen to him in the daytime too" (64). Of course, associating the subject matter with someone else is, for Freud, an unconscious admission of guilt; and just as he is about to suggest as much to Dora, she finally goes along with the program and admits that she used to wet her bed as a child. All of that work just to bring Dora to admit that she wet her bed as a child—resistance indeed!

In "Resistance and Repression," Freud tells his audience that resistance is not always "violent and tenacious"; it can also be "extremely subtle and often hard to detect" (*SE* 16:287). One subtle form is what Freud calls "intellectual resistance" (289). Intellectual resistance begins as a "violent and tenacious" rationalization: "It fights by means of arguments and exploits all the difficulties and improbabilities which normal but uninstructed thinking finds in the theories of analysis." Then, it takes a turn: "The patient is willing to be argued with; he is anxious to get us to instruct him, teach him, introduce him to the literature, so that he can find further instruction." Indeed, "he is quite ready to become an adherent of psycho-analysis." The overexuberance of the patient, intricately demonstrated by an interest and curiosity in what psychoanalysis has to say, is, as Freud astutely discerns, resistance, and therefore the analyst must repel it.

Resistance, indeed, "exhibits protean changes" (287), resulting in a wide spectrum of strategies. To demonstrate just how protean, Freud uses the example of the patient's reaction to the rule of free association. The fundamental rule in the psychoanalytic process is to say anything and everything that comes to mind without censor. "We urge him," Freud explains, "always to follow only the surface of his consciousness and not to leave aside any criticism of what he finds, whatever shape that criticism may take." Inevitably and invariably, this rule is violated—every violation constituting a flare of resistance.

> At one moment he declares that nothing occurs to him, at the next that so many things are crowding in on him that he cannot get hold of anything. . . . He then admits that there is something he really cannot say. . . . Or he says that something has occurred to him, but it concerns another person and not himself and is therefore exempt from being reported. Or, what has now occurred to him is really too unimportant, too silly and senseless. . . . So it goes on in innumerable variations, and one can only reply that "to say everything" really does mean "to say everything." (288)

Indeed, there is not one standard way of resisting but an entire assortment of strategies. The possible permutations are so infinite that it is better to say, as Freud does, that a resistance is simply "whatever interrupts the progress of analytic work" (555). Or, another way of putting it is to say that resistance is anything that interrupts, silences, or ignores the unconscious.

V

The goal of enabling a true exchange between the subject and the Other of the unconscious is not served by didactically enumerating what the analyst discerns is the knowledge stored in the unconscious. Though such didacticism might be useful—even necessary—at times, it cannot be the primary mode of analytic work since the analysand will only resist the content being transmitted. Rather, the analyst must prepare the exchange by disarming the analysand of the various strategies of resistance. Dora serves as an exemplary case. We already know that Dora's claim to not remember is, for Freud, an admission that a wealth of traumatic knowledge is possessed but unconscious. Dora's not-knowing is, as Freud would say, a not-wanting-to-know. The follies in her treatment mostly stem from Freud trying to didactically direct Dora in a desired course (for example, the setup with the matchbox), all of which she resists. It would be pointless for Freud to explain what traumatic knowledge is being spoken of by the unconscious unless Dora first relinquishes her strategies of resistance. Overcoming these strategies, and not didacticism, must be the work of analysis.

While it is pointless to identify every single possible strategy of resistance, at least one bears further explanation. In a very early paper, "The Neuro-Psychoses of Defence," written in 1894, Freud theorizes the origin of the defensive conflict thus:

> For these patients whom I analyzed had enjoyed good mental health up to the moment at which *an occurrence of incompatibility took place in their ideational life*—that is to say, until their ego was faced with an experience, an idea or a feeling which aroused such a distressing affect that the subject decided to forget about it because he had no confidence in his power to resolve the contradiction between that incompatible idea and his ego by means of thought-activity. (*SE* 3:47, original emphasis)

Here, Freud traces the inadmissibility of the unconscious to its incompatibility with the ego. The unconscious represents a threat to the ego, and therefore it defends itself against that threat by forcing the subject to "forget" traumatic knowledge. Later, in the "Resistance and Repression" lecture, Freud extends this line of thought to resistance as such: "In investigating resistance we have learnt that *it emanates from forces of the ego*, for known and latent character traits" (*SE* 16:298, emphasis added). Note the exceptionalism Freud reserves for the ego: he does not describe the ego as one specific form of resistance; rather, he suggests it is the source of all the strategies of resistance. In order to demonstrate how all resistance leads back to the ego, let us return to the Ratman. He tells Freud the following story about him and his brother:

> We both owned toy guns of a well-known type; I loaded mine using the ramrod and told him if he looked down the barrel he would see something interesting, and when he was looking down it, I pulled the trigger. I hit him in the forehead and did not do him any harm, but my intention was really to hurt him. Afterwards I was beside myself, threw myself on the ground asked myself: how could I possibly have done that?—But I did do it. (*Wolfman*, 147–48)

Clearly, the Ratman is upset with his intention to hurt his brother—indeed, to shoot him between the eyes. But what is the cause of his mood?—the incompatibility between the deed and the way the Ratman sees himself. In other words, the difference between the way he really is and the way he is in his ego. This dissonance becomes stronger when it comes to Freud's suggestion that the Ratman's traumatic knowledge revolves around wanting to kill his father: "He expressed doubt, however, that all his evil impulses have their origin in childhood" (148). Again, the Ratman resists the unconscious. Looking closely at the Ratman's denial reveals something very telling. The Ratman does not believe he could have made such a wish on the weak basis that it simply does not accord with his self-image: "Such thoughts amaze him [the Ratman], he tells me, since he is quite sure that his father's death is something he could never have wished for, but only feared" (144). He insists that Freud is wrong simply because such wishes go against the way he imagines himself to be, the way he styles himself—in short, his ego. Thus the ego—what we feel is the very seat of our identity and self-understanding—turns out to be the unconscious's strongest foe, the very source of all the strategies of resistance. For this reason, Lacan formulates his work as a tour de force against ego-psychology's privileging of the ego. In contrast to ego-psychology, Lacan states: "If there is an image which could represent for us the Freudian notion of the unconscious, it is indeed that of the acephalic subject, of a subject who no longer has an ego, who doesn't belong to the ego" (*S* II:167).

VI

Central to Lacan's critique of the ego is his groundbreaking essay "The Mirror Stage as Formative of the *I* Function."[9] In this essay, Lacan presents his most recognizable contribution to psychoanalytic theory: the theory of the so-called mirror-stage. According to this theory, sometime in early development—anywhere from the age of "six months on . . . up to the age of eighteen months" ("Mirror," 4)—the child is put in front of a mirror and is told of its reflection, "That's you!" For Lacan, this event is significant because it is the moment when the child first identifies with its mirror-image: "It suffices to understand the mirror stage in this context *as an identification,* in the full sense analysis gives to the term: namely, the transformation that takes place in the subject when he assumes an image" (4, original emphasis).[10] From the "jubilant assumption of his specular image," "the *I* is precipitated in a primordial form" (4). Lacan uses "*I*" in various ways, and what he means by it depends on the context in which he is using it. What is most important for the present purposes is to understand that saying "*I*" is how the subject is constituted. For Lacan, different, what might be called, agencies attempt to constitute themselves by announcing "*I*"—for example, the unconscious and the analysand's ego compete to announce themselves as "*I*" in the analytic situation. The subject announcing "*I*" in the case of the mirror-event is the child's ego, which is constituted by the identification between the child and its mirror-image. But this *I*-function, as we know, is imaginary or specular, and therefore, according to psychoanalysis, it cannot be the final word on the issue.

What Lacan finds unique about this mirror-experience is that it provides the child, who at this point has only a "fragmented image of the body," with an image of itself in the "'orthopedic' form of its totality" (6). In other words, the mirror-stage is the developmental stage in which the child first experiences itself as a whole. The experience of identifying with an image of its wholeness is profoundly empowering for the child. This child "who has not yet mastered walking, or even standing," now experiences total mastery over the body insofar as it is in full control of the movements of the reflection:

> For the total form of his body, by which the subject anticipates the maturation of his power in a mirage, is given to him only as a gestalt, that is, in an exteriority in which, to be sure, this form is more constitutive than constituted, but in which, above all, it appears to him as the contour of his stature that freezes it and in a symmetry that reverses it, in opposition to the turbulent movements with which the subject feels he animates it. (4)

However, any mastery the child experiences can only be imaginary because the child controls only its reflection, not its real body—the child is after all only about one year old. Identification with the mirror-image is always an imaginary relation. Sometime after the publication of the "Mirror Stage" essay, in his seminar on *Freud's Papers on Technique*, Lacan comments that the mirror-identification "gives the subject an imaginary mastery over his body, one which is premature in relation to a real mastery" (*S* I:79). Because it is based on an experience of mastery that is purely imaginary, "the agency known as the ego," which announces itself as "*I*," is set "in a fictional direction," thus predestining the subject to live in "discordance with his own reality" ("Mirror," 4). The subject constituted through the mirror-stage is condemned to always experience conflict between mastery in the imagination and the unruliness of the body itself.

Though the "Mirror Stage" essay ends on a down note, with the *I* emerging "in a fictional direction" as a purely imaginary ego, it is by far not Lacan's last word on these matters, and in seminar XI, he broaches it again. Lacan argues that the child's first experience with society is that of alienation because "the subject depends on the signifier," and "the signifier is first of all in the field of the Other" (*S* XI:205). Dependent upon the signifier because the child is first recognized by others through language—indeed, much of the linguistic constitution of the child, such as the name, occurs even before birth. The signifier is usually as simple as the child's name, but it can be as elaborate as all the social norms and expectations that go along with the signifier "boy" or "girl." In any case, for the child to be recognized in the symbolic order of society, it must accept its given signifier as its own. Accepting the signifier means being alienated by it because those signifiers are usually not of one's choosing. The child enters into intelligible social relations—that is, the field of the Other—but it is "eclipsed . . . by the very function of the signifier" (211). So the child must make a choice: either be alienated by the signifier and enter society or reject it and remain unrecognizable in social terms: "Alienation consists in this *vel*, which . . . condemns the subject to appearing only in that division which . . . appears on one side as meaning, produced by the signifier," and "on the other as *aphanisis*" (210), that is "disappearance" (207). Lacan's dialectic of alienation and aphanisis may appear obscure, but its terms are actually quite familiar ones: namely, it describes the dynamic of the mirror-stage. The child's identification with its reflection—designated with the signifiers, "That's you!"—is the alienation of its real existence by an idealized yet imaginary image: "Take just one signifier as an insignia of this omnipotence . . . and you have the unary trait which . . . alienates this subject in the first identification that forms the ego-ideal."[11] Aphanisis would then be the failure to identify with the reflection, which implies the total inability to function within "socially elaborated situations" ("Mirror," 7).

In a series of talks in seminar XI, under the heading "Of the Gaze as *Objet Petit a*," while considering the question of the human fascination with pictures, Lacan states the following:

I am taking the structure at the level of the subject here, and it reflects something that is already to be found in the natural relation that the eye inscribes with regard to light. I am not simply that punctiform being located at the geometral point from which the perspective is grasped. No doubt, in the depths of my eye, the picture is painted. The picture, certainly, is in my eye. But I am not in the picture. (*S* XI:96)

Though there is a lot happening in this passage, which can obscure Lacan's exact meaning, what is clear is that he is describing some kind of relationship between a picture and its viewer, a relationship of fascination. Notice what Lacan says in the end. No matter how dynamic this relationship of fascination is, it is clear that "I am not in the picture." Lacan seems to be pointing out the obvious, for no matter how narcissistic a person might be, only a fool would confuse themselves with an image in a picture. But wasn't there a time when the viewer in fact *did* confuse themselves with the image?—of course, the mirror-stage! Though Lacan here is discussing pictures, his comments should be read as extending the line of argument in the "Mirror Stage" essay. The ego set in a fictional or imaginary direction is not the end of the subject's constitution. The child is not in the picture, that is to say, the imaginary identification produced by the mirror-relation is not strong enough to encage the child forever. At some point, the child realizes "I am not in the picture." Lacan calls this addendum to his original mirror-theory, the theory of "separation" (214).

His talk on the picture continues:

That which is light looks at me, and by means of that light in the depths of my eye, something is painted—something that is not simply a constructed relation, the object on which the philosopher lingers—but something that is an impression, the shimmering of a surface that is not, in advance, situated for me in its distance. That is something that introduces what was elided in the geometral relation—the depth of field, with all of its ambiguity and variability, which is in no way mastered by me. (96)

Again, Lacan is difficult to follow as he is covering a lot of ground very quickly, but notice that in the end he states that there is something in a picture that is "in no way mastered by me." The mirror-stage was formative precisely because it afforded an experience of mastery, albeit illusory. What breaks the imaginary identification, what makes the child realize that "I am not in the picture," that is to say, what causes separation, is an object within the frame of the picture or mirror that resists mastery. Far from being mastered, this object actually "grasps me, solicits me at every moment" (96), insofar as it solicits or causes the viewer's desire to know what it is. This stubborn object in the picture thus causes separation while simultaneously acting as a "lure" (100) to captivate the viewer's attention. Lacan calls this object, the object *a* (in French, *objet petit a* or *objet a*), and "the *objet a* in the field of the visible is the gaze" (105), which, among many things, means that the picture literally looks at the viewer.

VII

We can now use Lacan's critique of the ego to further describe the dynamics of the analytic setting. The force that keeps the unconscious from being heard is the imaginary relation that the analysand constructs between their ego and the analyst's. To state it differently, the analysand enters into a mirror-relation with the analyst's ego. The analysand identifies with the analyst by grasping onto the ways they are similar. In a way, the analysand is saying to the analyst, "You are like me!" The analysand will even go so far as to be alienated by the analyst's ego: "After all," as the analysand seems to say, "the analyst is the trained professional, the expert." By regarding the analyst as a mirror-image of one's self results in attempts to master that image, the analyst. Returning for a moment to Dora—all of her resistance stems from her desire for mastery over Freud, which means the ego is at the bottom of the conflict. Dora is trying to maintain the integrity of her ego by mastering her image *qua* Freud.

For the unconscious to be heard, the ego must be muted. But one does *not* mute the ego by debasing, insulting, or shaming it; for indeed the ego will simply redouble itself against such efforts at traumatization. Rather, one disarms the ego by breaking the imaginary identification that alienates the analysand's subjectivity in the analyst's, that is, by causing separation. For this reason, Lacan says that the analyst must be "not a living mirror, but an empty mirror" (*S* II:246). The analyst must be a mirror that reflects an empty image, that is, an image with which the patient cannot identify. The analyst does so by functioning as object *a*, that obscure object which sullies a perfect picture. And the analyst functions this way by speaking on behalf of the unconscious—the true subject of psychoanalysis.

In many ways, the analyst must act heroically and ethically. For example: the analyst must diminish their ego in order to prevent identification; the analyst must stand up to the analysand's attempts to master the situation; and the analyst must advocate for the most unpopular voice in the room, that of the unconscious. Acting in this manner means the analyst must be an empty picture: not a picture that the analysand looks at but rather a picture that gazes back at the analysand with an invitation to hear the unconscious.

3

Transference or, When Discourses Shift: Toward a Theory of Psychopedagogical Technique

I

Psychoanalysis is a special kind of learning. Rather than simply being told of the knowledge stored in the unconscious, psychoanalysis insists that one must learn for oneself by overcoming the resistances one puts up to it. Freud explains psychoanalysis's unique status in perhaps the most important of the *Papers on Technique*, "Remembering, Repeating and Working-Through."[1] Freud begins the paper by reviewing the history of psychoanalysis's development. Early in its development, psychoanalysis simply wanted to bypass what Freud described as an overactive critical faculty. As psychoanalysis comes into its own, the analyst "employs the art of interpretation mainly for the purpose of recognizing the resistances which appear there, and making them conscious" (*SE* 12:147). "The aim of the different techniques," Freud insists, "has, of course, remained the same" (147–48): "Descriptively speaking, it is to fill in gaps in memory; dynamically speaking, it is to overcome resistances due to repression" (148).

Freud adds, "One must allow the patient time to become more conversant with this resistance with which he has now become acquainted, to *work through* it, to overcome it, by continuing, in defiance of it, the analytic work according to the fundamental rule of analysis" (155, original emphasis). Freud's warning is that simply recognizing the resistances is not enough; they must be disarmed or worked through. If not fully worked through, resistances will repeat, hindering analysis from making any progress. It may be true that this "working-through of the resistances may in practice turn out to be an arduous task for the subject of the analysis and a trial of patience for the analyst" (155). "Nevertheless," Freud goes on to say, "it is a part of the work which effects the greatest changes in the patient and which distinguishes analytic treatment from any kind of treatment by suggestion" (155–56). As integral as working-through is to psychoanalytic theory and practice, one can more accurately describe the educational theory implicit in psychoanalysis not so much as learning the traumatic knowledge of the unconscious as the very process of overcoming resistances.

II

In the years 1953–1954, Lacan gave the first of his famed seminars; the topic was *Freud's Papers on Technique*.[2] In this seminar, Lacan gives an exemplary case for the dangers of not heeding the words of Freud and ignoring the importance of working-through the resistances. His example comes via his polemic with the ego-psychologists, that group of psychoanalysts who sought to turn psychoanalysis into a mere psychology by replacing the centrality of the unconscious with the ego. Lacan wants to reveal the poverty of any attempt to treat the ego as a kind of bedrock rather than a resistance. To do so, he makes an example of one of the foundational ego-psychologists, Ernst Kris. Kris, whose version of psychoanalysis Lacan later calls "crass" (*S* II:113), gives an account of a patient who happens to be a scholar. The scholar's "life is as it were fettered by the feeling he has of being . . . a plagiarist" (*S* I:59). This feeling that' he is always plagiarizing plagues Kris's patient, even preventing him from publishing. "All the same," Lacan recounts, "he manages to get one text into shape" (60).

But, one day, he turns up declaring almost triumphantly that the whole of his thesis is already to be found in the library, in a published article. So there he is, this time, a plagiarist despite himself. . . . Kris in actual fact gets interested in what happened and what the article contains. Looking into it more closely, he realizes that none of the central theses brought forward by the subject are to be found there.

On Kris's diagnosis, the scholar's symptom stems from a weak ego inherited from his father, who "never succeeded in producing anything, because he was crushed by a grandfather." Lacan does not quarrel with Kris's diagnosis—indeed, he claims: "There's no question about it, the interpretation is valid." What Lacan contests is Kris's method of treatment. Instead of treating the feeling of having plagiarized as a resistance and working through it, Kris merely wants to rehabilitate the scholar's ego by showing him the differences between the two articles thus didactically proving to him that no plagiarism has in fact taken place. Kris's idea is this: once the scholar sees the objective fact that his article is not plagiarized, he will regain confidence and thus develop a stronger ego. Confronted by Kris, the scholar cannot deny the veracity of the diagnosis. On Kris's theory, the scholar should be cured at the moment of recognition. While it is true that the scholar no longer seems haunted by feelings of plagiarism, he says something very strange at his next session; Lacan paraphrases it thus: "The other day, on leaving, I went into such and such street . . . and I sought out a place where I could find the dish I am particularly fond of, fresh brains." By not working through the resistance—a process that would ultimately confront and overcome the ego itself—the resistance returns, this time in the form of an appetite for brains.

The arduous working-through of resistances often manifests as a struggle between analyst and analysand as "unconscious impulses do not want to be remembered in the way the treatment desires them to be" (*SE* 12:108). "This struggle between the doctor and the patient, between intellect and instinctual life, between understanding and seeking to act," as Freud explains, "is played out almost exclusively in the phenomena of transference." Its function as the theatre in which these struggles are played out also makes the transference the strongest tool for overcoming the resistances. "It cannot be disputed that controlling the phenomena of transference presents the psycho-analyst with the greatest difficulties," Freud admits. "But," he goes on, "it should not be forgotten that it is precisely they that do us the inestimable service of making the patient's hidden and forgotten erotic impulses immediate and manifest," which is why Freud says: "It is on that field that the victory must be won."

III

Overcoming or working through the resistances, in Lacan, always results in a shift in the way individuals relate to each other within the given learning situation. Lacan's theory of the four discourses, the subject of seminar XVII, *The Other Side of Psychoanalysis*,[3] offers an elaborate model for thinking through the kinds of shifts that are possible. Before turning to the four discourses themselves, it is important to clarify that by "discourse" Lacan does not mean language, talk, or speech per se. "The fact is, in truth," Lacan states at the outset of seminar XVII, "discourse can clearly subsist without words" (13). Lacan even calls his concept of discourse a "discourse without speech" (12). What he wants to designate with the term "discourse" are the ways in which individuals are ordered and organized within a given social situation. In other words, discourse is, for Lacan, structure: "This is like an *apparatus*. You should, at least, get the idea that it could be used as a lever, as a pair of pliers, that it can be screwed down, assembled in one way or another" (169, emphasis added). In *Encore*, Lacan sharpens his use of discourse, describing it as a "social link" (*S* XX:54). If Lacan retains the phrase "discourse," it is because social beings are, for him, always linked in and through language:

> [Discourse] subsists in certain fundamental relations which would literally not be able to be maintained without language.

Through the instrument of language a number of stable relations are established, inside which something that is much larger
and goes much further than actual utterances can, of course, be
inscribed.

(*S* XVII:13)

So, while individuals qua speaking beings do indeed talk to one
another, Lacan is describing the larger social relations, structures, or links binding them together through that linguistic
medium. Thus, the four discourses do not simply describe four
ways of talking but, more fundamentally, four ways of relating
socially.

The four discourses are shown graphically by the four basic
terms—S_1, S_2, \$, *a*—occupying places within the general schema
shown in Figure 3.1.

The four basic terms are written as abstract notations so that
their meaning can vary according to the role associated with
the place each occupies within the general schema, as Lacan
explains: "It's no accident if I have given only these little letters
here. It's because I do not want to put things up that might give
the appearance of signifying. I do not at all want to signify them,
but to authorize them" (169). However, a starting point may
be helpful; so take S_1, S_2, \$, and *a* to provisionally mean, respec-
tively, the alienating master signifier (see Chapter 2), knowledge,
the (barred) subject, and the surplus object.

The first of the four discourses, what Lacan calls the master's
discourse, appears when these terms take the initial positions
represented in Figure 3.2.

Here, the master (S_1) is shown lording over the slave (S_2),
forcing the latter to work and produce an object. In the master's
discourse, the master does not so much impose its knowledge
upon the slave as force the slave to produce knowledge for it: "It is

Agent   ⟶   Other

Truth   Production

Figure 3.1   The basic scheme of the four discourses

$$\frac{S_1}{\$} \xrightarrow{M} \frac{S_2}{a}$$

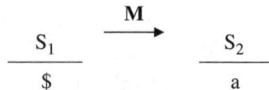

Figure 3.2   The master's discourse

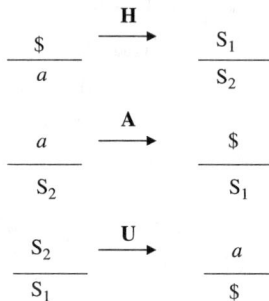

$$\frac{\$}{a} \xrightarrow{H} \frac{S_1}{S_2}$$

$$\frac{a}{S_2} \xrightarrow{A} \frac{\$}{S_1}$$

$$\frac{S_2}{S_1} \xrightarrow{U} \frac{a}{\$}$$

Figure 3.3   The discourse of the hysteric, the analyst, and the university

all about finding the position that makes it possible for knowledge to become the master's knowledge" (22). One might say that, in the master's discourse, the only knowledge that receives recognition as knowledge is that which is sanctioned by a higher authority. Knowledge is produced, in other words, solely for the master's enjoyment. The truth of this discourse is that no learning happens at all insofar as the master does not care if the knowledge is accurate but only that it works: "A real master . . . doesn't desire to know anything at all—he desires that things work" (24). For this reason, the master is, for Lacan, in truth, always a "birdbrain" (38).

The three remaining discourses are generated by giving the master's discourse a quarter-turn, which are shown in Figure 3.3.

It should be noted that giving the initial schema a quarter-turn does not imply a formal sequence or order: "My little quadrupedal schemas . . . are not the Ouiji boards of history. It is not necessarily the case that things always happen this way, and that things rotate in the same direction" (188). Rather, they map the relations that exist within any given social situation: "This is only an appeal for you to locate yourselves in relation to what one can call radical functions, in the mathematical sense of the term" (188). Lacan, however, does suggest that the university's discourse—produced by giving the master's schema a quarter-turn counterclockwise—while not a logical consequence, is still very much akin to the master's discourse, even going so far as to call it the "discourse of the perverted master" (182). In the university's discourse, knowledge (S_2) is in the dominant position. Here, knowledge is efficiently produced. However, the knowledge at stake in the university's discourse is "not knowledge of everything," Lacan says, "but all-knowing . . . which in ordinary language is called the bureaucracy" (31). Like in the master's discourse, the concerned knowledge is not true but efficient knowledge, bureaucratized knowledge. The bureaucracy is, in truth, another, more modern, master: "One could thus write that what is the S_1 in the master's discourse can be said to be congruent with, or equivalent to, what comes and functions as S_2 in the university's discourse" (102). What the university's discourse so efficiently produces with its bureaucratized knowledge is "a thinking being, a subject" (174), an effort that "extends much further back, back to the level of the master's discourse" (174–75). But these are not creative subjects who actively make living knowledge; rather, they are automatons, filled with the university's dead information: "As subject, in its production, there is no question of it being able to see itself for a single instant as the master of knowledge" (174). Therefore, if the university's discourse is educational, then it is a highly bureaucratic education in which knowledge is controlled, regulated, and prescribed.

Turning the master's discourse one quarter the other way produces, what Lacan calls, the hysteric's discourse. The hysteric's discourse is a kind of reversal of the master's: here, the hysteric rejects the master, "goes on a kind of strike" (94), and rebels against its authority. The hysteric's rebellion is, in many ways, caused by the various forms of subjugation suffered in the master's and university's discourses. Subordinated, the hysteric knows the truth of these discourses of mastery, and "this truth, to say it at last, is that the master is castrated" (97), that is, undeserving of its symbolic role. By rising to the position of agent, the hysteric wants to make this truth known by undermining the master's position. But undermining is not the same as nullifying, and so, what matters to the hysteric is not that the master's function disappears but that it "produces knowledge. And not just any knowledge—knowledge about the truth" (97), all of which the hysteric will, of course, once again, undermine. If the hysteric's discourse actually preserves the master's function, then what does the hysteric truly want?—"What the hysteric wants," Lacan claims, "is a master" (129). The hysteric, that is to say, "wants a master she can reign over. She reigns, and he does not govern" (129).

The last of the four discourses is the discourse of the analyst. The "Other Side" [*L'Envers*] in the title of seminar XVII refers to the way the analyst's discourse appears when the master's discourse is turned upside down. However, that the analyst's discourse is the "other side" of the master's discourse "does not mean that it resolves" (54) it—indeed, the analyst's discourse, Lacan cautiously states, "doesn't resolve anything." The analyst's discourse is the other side of the master's in that it is a discourse of *nonmastery*: "This is the difficulty faced by anyone whom I try to bring as close as I am able to the analyst's discourse—and who has to be located at the opposite of any wish, at least any declared wish, for mastery" (69). Rather than trying to master the irreducible representative of the unconscious (written here as *a*), the analyst's discourse structures relations in such a way that it causes there to be new knowledge of the unconscious. By endowing the unconscious with agency, the analyst's discourse sets itself apart not only from the master's but also from the other two discourses: whereas the master controls the slave, the bureaucracy controls knowledge, and the hysteric controls the master, the analyst controls nothing. The analyst is merely situated in the position of *a*, that is, as "the cause of desire" (152), in order to help the analysand understand—not control or defend—unconscious formations.

I will discuss how these four discourses describe different learning contexts in more detail below. At this point, I want to suggest that the discourse of the analyst is an educational discourse insofar as it is the only discursive formation in which the analysand learns from the unconscious and demonstrates this learning by producing traumatic knowledge. The analyst's pedagogy, on this account, aims at manipulating the various discourses that operate within the analytic context to produce this discursive formation: it facilitates the confronting and working-through of resistances, above all the ego, that stagnate the situation within the master's, the university's, or the hysteric's discourses. But how exactly does it affect this working-through? That is to ask, what, according to Lacan's theory, causes one discourse to turn into another? Lacan's answer comes obliquely: while revisiting the four discourses in *Encore*, he claims that "love is the sign that one is changing discourses" (*S* XX:16). Lacan's comment does not answer the question as much as reframe it. The question now becomes: what form does love take within psychoanalysis?—answer: the transference.

> The subject comes into play on the basis of this fundamental support—the subject is supposed to know, simply by virtue of being a subject of desire. Now what actually happens? What happens is what is called in its most common appearance the *transference effect*. This effect is love.
>
> (*S* XI:253, original emphasis)

The analyst's specific pedagogical skill is being able to handle the transference, which, handled correctly, results in shifts in the discursive underpinnings of the analytic situation; or, to put it another way, the transference is the foundational technique of psychoanalytic pedagogy.

IV

Freud describes transference as the "stereotype plate" (*SE* 12: 100) of the "preconditions to falling in love" (99) that is established early in development and "constantly repeated . . . in the course of the person's life" (100). Once formed, the "stereotype plate" is superimposed or *transferred* onto every new person met such that individuals are "bound to approach every new person . . . with libidinal anticipatory ideas" (100).

An excellent cinematic example of transference can be found in Alfred Hitchcock's masterpiece *Vertigo*.[4] In Hitchcock's *Vertigo*, Scottie (James Stewart), a former police officer suffering from acrophobia, falls in love with the troubled Madeleine (Kim Novak). After a series of fateful events, Madeleine plunges to her death. Scottie, however, remains obsessed with Madeleine. Then, he meets Judy Barton, who possesses a remarkable resemblance to Madeleine—indeed Judy and Madeleine are both played by Novak. Unable to let it go at a resemblance, Scottie forces Judy to further change her appearance to better align with Madeleine's. The more time they spend together, the more Scottie changes Judy's appearance, even forcing her to wear a blonde wig. In psychoanalytic terms, Scottie is transferring the "preconditions to falling in love" that he formed through his relationship with Madeleine onto Judy's person: that is to say, Scottie and Judy's relationship is transferential insofar as it is overdetermined by Scottie's "libidinal anticipatory ideas."

Freud observes that analytic treatment is always full of transference: that is to say, the analysand always meets the analyst with "libidinal anticipatory ideas" that are usually first formed in relation to a primary caregiver. The transference exhibited in analysis is so pronounced that Freud goes as far as to claim "it is provoked by the analytic situation" (*SE* 12:168) itself. Clearly, Freud believes his claim is modest because he presents it as if it were a matter of fact. But a good question to ask is: why does the analytic situation elicit the transference? Further confounding the issue is this: elsewhere, Freud admits the transference is not localized to analysis but can be observed in "other situations too" and is even a "common event in institutions" (106) as such. How then to reconcile on one hand the ubiquity of transference and on the other its intensification in analysis?

To answer these questions, let us now turn to Lacan. As I argued above, transference, in Lacan—as in Freud—is a relationship of love. However, Lacan further specifies that knowledge underwrites transference-love; he claims: "I love the person I assume to have knowledge" (*S* XX:67). It is now clear why the analytic situation elicits the transference: analysis is a situation of knowledge, namely, traumatic knowledge, which the analysand, at least initially, supposes the analyst knows. For Lacan, the analyst's credibility derives not from some external credentialing agency but from securing the "trust of a subject as such" (*S* XI:230). What Lacan means is that the analysand comes to analysis only because there is, on some level, trust that the analyst is knowledgeable in the ways of the unconscious. The analysand, in other words, enters the analytic situation having credited or *transferred* to the person of the analyst the title of, what Lacan calls, the "subject supposed to know" (232). The analyst's ability to elicit the analysand's trust in their abilities is what, in the analytic situations, provokes transference.

It should also be clear why Freud claims that the transference manifests in many institutions other than analysis. Almost every institution—the school, the church, the government, to name only a few—is, in some way, predicated on knowledge. To put it in Lacan's locution, all institutions operate on the assumption that a "subject supposed to know" exists. What elicits the transference is then not so much the institutions themselves as the way they organize knowledge. Strictly speaking, transference can exist beyond the boundaries of formal institutions—indeed anywhere knowledge is at stake: "As soon as the subject who is supposed to know exists somewhere . . . there is transference" (232).

The fact that it is full of transference does not necessarily present a problem for the course of analysis. Certainly, the transference can interfere with the progress of analysis if the analyst does not eventually deflect the position of "subject supposed to know." While the analyst is seen as the "subject supposed to know," Lacan cautions that no analyst actually *is* the "subject supposed to know" because "no psychoanalyst can claim to represent, in however slight a way, a corpus of absolute knowledge" (232). Therefore, the analyst's claim to that position must always be temporary and contingent. In the analytic situation, the only true "subject supposed to know" is the unconscious itself—as one of Lacan's translators, Bruce Fink, aptly puts it: "The unconscious . . . must be taken by the analyst to be the ultimate authority, the Other, the subject supposed to know."[5] While it is true that transference can impede the progress of analysis, it is the strongest tool at the analyst's disposal, if handled correctly. "The main instrument," Freud writes, "however, for curbing the patient's compulsion to repeat and for turning it into a motive for remembering lies in the handling of the transference" (SE 12:154). Lacan similarly states: "We are linked together in awaiting this transference effect in order to be able to interpret" (S XI:253). So, while the analyst must take care not to let it turn analysis awry, the transference must nevertheless be established.

Proper handling of the transference results in shifts in the discursive structure of the learning situation. As we will see, the discourse of the analyst emerges when the transference is finally overcome, that is, when the unconscious replaces the analyst as the "subject supposed to know." But because it is initiated with the analysand placing trust in the analyst's knowledge—that is to say, it begins with the analysand *transferring* the title of "subject supposed to know" to the analyst—"the analytic practice is, properly speaking, initiated by this master's discourse" (S XVII:152). That is because learning the traumatic knowledge of the unconscious is only possible when a *fundamental trust* is established between the analysand and the analyst. The analysand must be assured that the analyst, in fact, possesses the requisite knowledge for *guiding* the learning process that is psychoanalysis. In other words, the analysand must be able to transfer the position of "subject supposed to know" onto the analyst.

V

Establishing the transference—that is, establishing the master's discourse—is vital to the learning process that is psychoanalysis. It also presents a problem if held too long. Psychoanalysis, as Fink says, affirms that the unconscious is the final authority within the analytic situation. Thus the analyst's hold on the title of "subject supposed to know" must not be without a certain amount of irony, self-deprecation, and even a sense of humor. Remaining attached to this position can negatively result in two possible scenarios: first is identification and second is a shift to the hysteric's discourse.

"Identification," Freud writes, "is known to psycho-analysis as the earliest expression of an emotional tie with another person."[6] Furthermore, it is an emotional tie that "endeavours to mould a person's own ego after the fashion of the one that has been taken as a model" (*Group*, 48). Identification means that the analysand sees the analyst as a role model and thus strives to act and think in the latter's fashion. True, being a role model may not appear problematic, and it is indeed the role traditionally ascribed to any "subject supposed to know." But, for Freud, identification is problematic because in it the role model "enjoys a certain amount of freedom from criticism" (56). "The tendency which falsifies judgement in this respect," found at work in identification, "is that of *idealization*" (56, original emphasis). Identification is always accompanied by idealization. By acting as the master of knowledge, the analyst easily becomes a point of identification for the analysand. And once this happens, the analyst will be idealized, pushing the person of the analyst beyond criticism. Moreover, preoccupied with acting like the analyst, the analysand will never truly learn what the unconscious has to say. It is therefore important to further specify the transference as a rapport that is not identification. While both are a kind of rapport or love between analyst and analysand, identification is always accompanied by idealization. While the person who becomes the object of the transference fits within certain preconditions for love, that person—the transferential object, as it were—is not idealized. If anything, the transferential object can be criticized for not living up to the standard of the original object with which the stereotyped plate was first formed (as is the case in *Vertigo* between Scottie and Judy). The transference can thus be described as a kind of rapport-without-idealization.

On the one hand, if identification defines the situation, it will remain frozen within the master's discourse, and the analyst's various utterances will be taken by the analysand as oracles to be unconditionally accepted. On the other hand, if transference defines that situation, the analyst can then handle transference in such a way as to shift the focus onto the unconscious.

Remaining in the master's position can also have the opposite effect: it can incur the analysand's ire, thus causing a shift to the hysteric's discourse. "The hysteric's discourse," Lacan claims, "reveals the master's discourse's relationship to *jouissance*," or intense pleasure, "in the sense that in it knowledge occupies the place of *jouissance*" (*S* XVII:94). Lacan can be taken as meaning that the hysteric finds out that the master is not concerned with learning per se but with taking pleasure in the very act of espousing knowledge itself. Speaking knowledge affords the master with a certain amount of "satisfaction of speech" (*S* XX:64). The master is not a true master of knowledge but someone who literally enjoys hearing their own talk. The hysteric "refuses to make himself its body" (*S* XVII:94), that is, refuses to play the role of sounding board for the master's chatter. In this negative turn of the transference, the hysteric derides the master, mocks the master's pretentiousness, and makes a game of poking holes in the master's knowledge. The hysteric's discourse is not as much the learner's liberation from the master's authority as a kind of reversal of positions: the hysteric becomes master. Underneath all of the hysteric's derision, Lacan detects an unwavering faith that a true master exists somewhere. The hysteric's problem is not with the position of master itself but with this particular person's claim to it. As for the function of master itself, the hysteric, Lacan cautions, "remains united" (94) with it. Thus the ultimate travesty of this mishandling of the transference is that it is fated to repeat the master's discourse—as Lacan famously told the student protestors: "What you aspire to as revolutionaries is a master. You will get one" (207).

To avoid both identification and the hysteric's discourse (or, in Freud's language, negative transference), the analyst must vacate the position of "subject supposed to know" and shift the focus to the unconscious itself. Affecting such a shift requires collaboration with the analysand to work through or overcome any relation that fixes the analyst to that position. For example, neophytes often believe that experts are responsible for providing content knowledge, but this belief has no real basis. Yet it is a belief that individuals have been socialized into holding from a very early age (Freud would say from as early as childhood) and for that reason has become recalcitrant. Overcoming this belief takes much work and involves a long, arduous process of helping novices understand that they are the ones who possess knowledge and are ultimately responsible for their own learning, not some so-called expert.

VI

There are of course many forms or strategies of resistance, but the relation or bond that presents the strongest impediment to the unconscious is, of course, the transference itself insofar as it is predicated upon the existence of the "subject supposed to know." For that reason, the transference itself must ultimately be overcome. Lacan calls this overcoming the "liquidation of the transference" (S XI:267). As the transference is liquidated, the discourse of the analyst emerges.

The most powerful tool for liquidating the transference and causing a shift to the analyst's discourse is what Lacan refers to as the analyst's desire. The analyst's desire is, in a certain way, the foundation and motor-force of transference. Lacan cannot stress this point enough, describing it as "the axis, the pivot, the handle, the hammer . . . the inertia, that lies behind . . . the transference" (235). The simplest way to use the tool of the analyst's desire is to ask questions: "What does this mean?" "Can you tell me?" "What do you think?" and so on. Or, to make brief leading statements: "Tell me more," "Very interesting," "You're on to something," and so on. Or, even, to express a lack of knowledge: "I have never thought of it that way," "I want to know more," and so on. Rather than showing incompetence, the analyst's desire signals that the analyst is not a master, not all knowing. Desire is a sign that the analyst is renouncing the position of "subject supposed to know." In relinquishing this title, space is created for the analysand's own desire to come into play in the form of *desiring to know what the analyst desires to know*: "Concerning the position called that of the analyst . . . it's as identical with the object *a*, that is to say with what presents itself for the subject as the cause of desire . . . insofar as it sets out on the trace left by the desire to know" (*S* XVII:106). Lacan explains: "The analyst makes himself the cause of the analysand's desire" (38). Functioning as the cause of the other's desire is the defining role the analyst plays within the analyst's discourse: "This is where the analyst positions himself. He positions himself as the cause of desire" (152). The conduit, in the analyst's discourse, that links these desires is the (liquidating) transference: "Behind the love known as transference, is the affirmation of the link between the desire of the analyst and the desire of the patient" (*S* XI:254).

Encountering the analyst's desire turns the analysand into a learner insofar as there becomes a desire to know what the other wants to know. So, what indeed does the analyst desire to know?—the answer is, of course, quite simple: the traumatic knowledge stored in the unconscious. Acting as the cause of desire, the analyst's desire directs the analysand as learner to the unconscious. And the more in tune these learners become with the unconscious, the less need there is for the guidance of the analyst's desire until finally the transference is totally liquidated and the unconscious has come fully into the position of "subject supposed to know."

When interjecting desire, the analyst must take care not to allow it to be pinned down to anything specific. The analyst's desire must always remain elusive to prevent identification. Yet, while it must not be attached to anything concrete, Lacan is careful to say that the "analyst's desire is not a pure desire. It is a desire to obtain absolute difference, a desire which intervenes when, confronted with the primary signifier, the subject is, for the first time, in a position to subject himself to it" (276). The analyst's desire is not pure, because it is partial toward the unconscious. It obtains absolute difference in two ways: first, because it differentiates the person of the analyst from the position of "subject supposed to know" and, second, because it dissolves the imaginary relation thus separating analyst and analysand. Lacan continues: "There only may the signification of a limitless love emerge, because it is outside the limits of the law, where alone it may live." In what way does the liquidation of the transference signify a "limitless love"? At the final stages of the psychoanalytic learning process, when the transference is finally liquidated, the "psychoanalyst typically extracts himself" (*S* XVII:185), leaving the analysand alone to learn directly from the unconscious itself. The analyst's final act is to remove every last trace of their presence, including desire, from the situation so that the analysand may finally become a student of the unconscious. This act of self-extraction so that learning may go forward is an act of love.

Liquidating the transference is, as Freud and Lacan claim, a long and arduous process, and there will inevitably be times when the analysand refuses to follow the analyst's desire. The reasons are various: for fear of being ashamed, in rebellion to authority, out of arrogance, and so on. Freud's case studies display the full range of possible reasons. At these moments, it is vital that the analyst not fall into the temptation of abandoning desire. Rather than withdraw, the analyst must redouble the commitment to desire. The analyst's persistence in desire constitutes a kind of ethical position: "From an analytical point of view, the only thing of which one can be guilty is of having given ground relative to one's desire" (*S* VII:319).

Excursus

Having engaged in a lengthy discussion of the pedagogical implications of psychoanalysis, I want to conclude this "Prolegomena" by embarking on an excursus to apply these ideas to the other kinds of pedagogical situations. What I want to suggest is that in other kinds of pedagogical situations—for example, the classroom of formal schooling—the analyst's desire manifest most concretely as ignorance. To make this claim, I rely upon the work of Jacques Ranciere, whose book, *The Ignorant Schoolmaster*,[7] presents the most thorough philosophical account of ignorance to date.

Ranciere's book recounts the career of one Joseph Jacotot, a Frenchman living in exile, as a professor, in the Netherlands. During his time in exile, Jacotot has what Ranciere describes as an "intellectual adventure,"[8] started by a philosophical experiment. A group of Flemish-speaking students ask Jacotot to teach them French. The only problem is that Jacotot does not speak Flemish. To teach them, the "minimal link of a *thing in common*," other than language, "had to be established between himself and them" (2, original emphasis). This link is a translated edition of *Telemaque*. Jacotot simply assigns the students to study this book until they are able to recite it. "He had communicated nothing to them about his science, no explications of the roots and the flexions of the French language" (9), Ranciere explains.

> He had left them alone with the text by Fenelon, a translation—not even interlinear like a schoolbook—and their will to learn French. He had only given them the order to pass through a forest whose openings and clearings he himself had not discovered. Necessity had constrained him to leave his intelligence entirely out of the picture.

And yet without the lead of the teacher's intelligence, "the fact was that his students had learned to speak and to write in French without the aid of explication."

The extraordinary result gives Jacotot a revelation: "One could learn by oneself and without a master explicator when one wanted to, propelled by one's own desire or by the constraint of the situation" (12). Learning and understanding are, for Jacotot, akin to translating a text in that they both are "giving the equivalent of a text" (9). And this work of giving equivalents or making analogies does not require the expertise of a master, only "the will to express" (10).

Now, this revelation strikes Jacotot as counterintuitive since "he had believed what all conscientious professors believe," namely, "that the important business of the master is to transmit his knowledge to his students so as to bring them, by degrees, to his own level of expertise" (3). The essential method for such transmission is explication, that is to say, "leading those minds, according to an ordered progression, from the most simple to the most complex." Due to his experiment, Jacotot is forced to rethink what he took as commonsense:

> Consider, for example, a book in the hands of a student. The book is made up of a series of reasonings designed to make a student understand some material. But now the schoolmaster opens his mouth to explain the book. He makes a series of reasonings in order to explain the series of reasonings that constitute the book. But why should the book need such help? Instead of paying for an explicator, couldn't a father simply give the book to his son and the child understand directly the reasonings of the book?
>
> (4)

There is a certain redundancy involved in the work of explication: the teacher explains the book, which itself is explaining some content. If explication calls for more explication, then does not someone need to explain the teacher's explication? But then that third explication would call for a fourth, and so on: "So the logic of explication calls for the principle of a regression ad infinitum: there is no reason for the redoubling of reasonings ever to stop."

Ranciere calls this circular argument: the explicative order. And, for Ranciere, more is at stake in it than a problematic methodology. At stake is the very principle of the equality of all people, for to "explain something to someone is first of all to show him he cannot understand it by himself" (6). The explicative order "divides intelligence into two" (7). "It says that there is an inferior intelligence," those who need explaining, "and a superior one," those who do the explaining. Simply put, some people are ignorant—those are the students. Others are knowledgeable—those are the teachers. To close this gap, teachers eliminate the other's ignorance by transmitting knowledge through explanation. But if the explicative order is predicated on there being a fundamental inequality of intelligences, then it cannot actually eliminate this inequality without dissolving itself; and so it does not:

> The Old Master says that a child's memory is incapable of such efforts because powerlessness, in general, is its slogan. It says that memory is something other than intelligence or imagination and, in so doing, it uses an ordinary weapon against those that want to prevail over powerlessness: division. It believes memory to be weak because it doesn't believe in the power of human intelligence. It believes it inferior because it believes in inferiors and superiors. In the end its double argument amounts to this: there are inferiors and superiors; inferiors can't do what superiors can.
>
> (24)

The explicative order is plagued by a perverse economy in which there is a surplus of both knowledge and ignorance in circulation. Teachers always possess too much knowledge, and students always possess too much ignorance. Thus, the inequality that separates their intelligences is never overcome. Ranciere puts it this way:

> Fragments add up, detached pieces of an explicator's knowledge that put the student on a trail, following a master with whom he will never catch up. The books is never whole, the lesson is never finished. The master always keeps a piece of learning—that is to say, a piece of the student's ignorance—up his sleeve. . . . The master is always a length ahead of the student, who always feels that in order to go farther he must have another master, supplementary explications.
>
> (21)

Instead of educating the student, the teacher links the student to their own intelligence—rather than that of the material itself—which, Ranciere argues, *stultifies* the student: "A person . . . may need a master when his own will is not strong enough to set him on track and keep him there. But that subjection is purely one of will over will. It becomes stultification when it links an intelligence to another intelligence" (13).

"The revelation that came to Joseph Jacotot amounts to this: the logic of the explicative system had to be overturned" (6).

Those who are considered ignorant in the explicative order must be emancipated as it were, and ushered into a new circle, which Ranciere calls the circle of power. In the circle of power, the ignorant teach themselves by "becoming conscious of his nature as an intellectual subject" (35), and being "obliged to use his own intelligence" (15). Through his experiment, Jacotot felicitously established the circle of power, and in it "the student was linked to a will, Jacotot's, and to an intelligence, the book's—the two entirely distinct" (13). No longer compared with Jacotot's intelligence, teacher and student met each other "not as students or as learned men, but as people; in the way you respond to someone speaking to you and not to someone examining you," that is, "under the sign of equality" (11).

Jacotot inaugurates this new circle of power with his one lesson: "I must teach you that I have nothing to teach you" (15). Jacotot comes to the situation in ignorance. His gesture is subtractive rather than additive. That is to say, if the problem with explicative order is a surplus of (the teacher's) knowledge and (the student's) ignorance, then Jacotot solves it not by introducing more knowledge but by "leaving his intelligence out of the picture" (13), that is, subtracting his intelligence, thus allowing the students' "intelligence to grapple with that of the book." Coming to them as ignorant, Jacotot introduces a new division of educational labor: from that moment, learning content is the sole power and responsibility of the student; the teacher's role is to strengthen the will.

The kind of situation Ranciere describes in Jacotot shares many affinities with psychoanalysis. In the situation set up by Jacotot, the book—not the teacher—serves as the intelligence that matters. The teacher and the student are connected only insofar as they are both interested in learning the book; it serves as "the egalitarian intellectual link between master and student." Likewise, in psychoanalysis, the unconscious—not the analyst—is ultimately the "subject supposed to know." Thus, the analyst, like Ranciere's ignorant schoolmaster, must provide an expertise other than knowledge. Jacotot provides strength of will, and the analyst provides desire. In order to let the other intelligence speak, both analyst and teacher must extract their intelligence from the situation. They both must teach that they have nothing to teach, that some other intelligence must be heard. Or, to put it in psychoanalytic terms, both analyst and teacher must vacate the position of "subject supposed to know." These homologies are represented in Figure 3.4.

Considering these resonances, it is not surprising that both Freud and Ranciere describes their processes—psychoanalysis and learning, respectively—as acts of *translation*: where Ranciere writes, "Learning and understanding are two ways of expressing the same act of translation (10), Freud writes, "It is of course only as something conscious that we know it, after it has undergone transformation or translation into something conscious. Psycho-analytic work shows us every day that translation of this kind is possible" (*SE* 14:166).

Interjecting analytic desire is thus a negative—not a positive—gesture. What is meant by this is that nothing is added but rather something is taken out: namely, the teacher's intelligence—hence, its appearance in the form of ignorance. It should be clear that the difference between the ignorant schoolmaster and the stultifying teacher is not dispositional. The ignorant schoolmaster is not kinder towards the students than the stultifying teacher. In fact, for Ranciere, the opposite is almost always the case:

> The stultifier is not an aged obtuse master who crams his students' skulls of poorly digested knowledge, or a malignant character mouthing half-truths in order to shore up his power

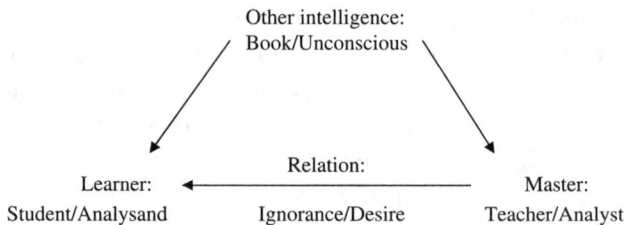

Figure 3.4 Discursive relations of Ranciere and Lacan

and the social order. On the contrary, he is all the more effica-
cious because he is knowledgeable, enlightened, and of good
faith.

(7)

The true difference between these two figures is structural: one
assumes the position of the ignorant, while the other assumes
the position of the "subject supposed to know." The ultimate
pedagogical act is thus always to remove the teacher's intelligence so that the other intelligence can be heard.

Part II

Secondary Revisions

4

Wo es war: Marxism, the Unconscious, and Subjectivity

I

Learning, at its most basic, can be described as the process of acquiring knowledge. Perhaps, with this definition's most standard and ordinary rendition, learning appears rather unproblematic for any conception of what it means to be a student—even coalescing with the latter. Thus a student, in the standard model, is simply the actor or subject who acquires knowledge—a happy union indeed. But does such a concept of subjectivity accord with a critical education? The question arises because what makes learning critical usually turns on the registering of some socially traumatic knowledge. In the various critical theories (feminist theory, Marxism, critical race theory, and the like), this traumatic knowledge goes by such names as exploitation, oppression, subjugation, and so on. When it comes to knowledge of the disturbing kind, can we continue to assume an unproblematic homology between learning and studenthood? In other words, do students easily or willfully learn knowledge that is traumatic—for example, knowledge of social and political oppression, acts of genocide, or economic exploitation?[1]

Even a cursory examination of the various modes of communication, from the cultural industry to schooling, will show that learning traumatic knowledge does not proceed without some resistance. It is enough to recall that the culture industry exists precisely to provide relief from social trauma, much less to help in knowing it. In that case, traumatic knowledge—the very knowledge at stake in critical theory—represents, from the standpoint of pedagogy, something of a problem for critical theory itself. Though endemic to all the various critical theories, where this problem is perhaps most pronounced is in Marxism. After all, Marx's very project, at its most narrow, was to demonstrate how exploitation was not avoidable collateral for capitalism but part of its integral structure, its very underside, that is, how the accumulation of capital is only possible if human misery also increases. Indeed, of capitalism's fundamental law, Marx writes in *Capital*: "It makes an accumulation of misery a necessary condition, corresponding to the accumulation of wealth."[2] And, at its broadest, his project was to confront the bourgeois metaphysics of surplus. Instead of serving as the basis for political mobilization, it seems more plausible that the traumatic knowledge discovered by Marx generates resistance— usually referred to as "ideology"—from capitalist subjects.

The question is this: if the knowledge we are concerned with is traumatic (as it is in Marxism), then, what is the corresponding notion of studenthood? It is within the context of this question that psychoanalysis offers itself as a suggestive contributor.[3] For psychoanalysis has always concerned itself with trauma and its subsequent repression; but, perhaps, more saliently, psychoanalysis attempts to project a model of subjectivity predicated on traumatic knowledge. Psychoanalysis will then be what adds the necessary facet to the Marxian prism— this is the articulation that will be sketched out here.

II

First entry can be made into this problematic by examining the philosophical presuppositions underpinning the standard model of studenthood. What one finds from such an examination is that the student as actor who acquires knowledge is modeled after none other than the Cartesian theory of subjectivity, that is, the cogito, "the thing that thinks."[4] It is not difficult to find Cartesian imprints in contemporary educational thought. We need only look as far as its two most prominent figures: John

Dewey and Paulo Freire.[5] In Dewey, we find the silhouette of a Cartesian structure in his appeal to reconstruct modern United States education on a more student-centered model. Driving Dewey, here, is his conception of the student as an active thinker/learner—or, translated into Cartesian terms, the subject of the student is a "thing" that exists by thinking experientially. As for Freire, in his famous problem-posing mode of education, the student is no longer an object filled by the teacher like so many empty buckets; rather, the student is now the active agent who comes to life by acts of cognition. "Liberating education," Freire writes, "consists in acts of cognition, not transferrals of information."[6] Again, Descartes is writ large in Freire's work as the student, according to the latter's account, is seen as a being who thinks, thus rendering any attempt to impose knowledge on the student from the outside an act of inhumanity.

Descartes' endeavor itself is well known: the fateful decision to cast doubt on all the knowledge he possesses, to effectively assume it to be so many lies, and to find instead a more substantial ground on which to assuredly fix the existence of his being. How does Descartes locate this desired ground? Through the course of doubting all his possessed knowledge, treating it as a collection of myths and fairytales, Descartes discovers that the only thing he can be certain of is that, insofar as he actively doubts, he is in fact thinking. Empty of all content, the act of thinking itself is christened as the grounds for being's certainty. Hence, the *I* is "a thing that thinks"—cogito—and therefore exists—ergo sum.

It is quite understandable that Cartesian subjectivity would serve as the model for ontologies of the student—indeed Descartes' methodological doubt is provocative in this regard. After all, Descartes himself did intend his *Mediations on First Philosophy* to be a didactic text on proper thinking. And when it comes to knowledge with which we are familiar and thus inclined to accept, the Cartesian method of doubt proves handy for creating a critical distance between the thinking *I* and its knowledge. But we are here concerned with traumatic knowledge—that is to say, knowledge not so easily accepted.

Traumatic knowledge is at stake in Marx's analysis of the mode of production insofar as what he has to tell us about capitalism is not easy to digest. "If now," Marx writes in his pamphlet "Wage Labour and Capital," "we picture to ourselves this feverish simultaneous agitation on the *whole world market,* it will be comprehensible how the growth, accumulation and concentration of capital results in an uninterrupted division of labour, and in the application of new and the perfecting of old machinery precipitately and on an ever more gigantic scale."[7] The key to Marx's insight here is "simultaneity"—that is, the necessity to grasp, in a single motion, all sides of capital accumulation, which means the ability to picture its over- and undersides as a single totality. The overside of capitalism is obviously its various productivities: wealth, commodities, etc. These are easy enough to imagine (and desire) and therefore present no problem to any student interested in studying capitalism—indeed these things suggest themselves as candidates for Cartesian doubt. The underside however is not so inviting. It is of course the necessity of human misery. As we saw above, for Marx, to recognize misery as the underside of capitalism is therefore to understand the fundamental law of capitalist accumulation.

The difficulty Marx's analysis of capitalism presents to any Cartesian model of student subjectivity is that the knowledge of human misery is not something we carry with us uncritically. Indeed, it is not difficult to find apologists who even today deny that capitalism produces misery as an essential part of its operation. Rather, misery is knowledge we do not yet fully comprehend or, more exactly, *want* to comprehend. As Freud might put it, the not-knowing of misery is more or less a conscious not-wanting-to-know. An even more radical example can be found in Marx's historical reconstruction of so-called primitive accumulation at the end of *Capital.* "So-called primitive accumulation," Marx writes, "therefore, is nothing else than the historical process of divorcing the producer from the means of production" (*Capital,* 874–75). Historically, this process of divorce is one where "conquest, enslavement, robbery, murder, in short, force play the greatest part" (875). The thrust of Marx's reconstruction is how it exposes the bourgeois political economists of his time as not willing to accept that "capital comes," into the world, "dripping from head to toe, from every pore, with blood and dirt" (926).

To accept that capital emerges "dripping from head to toe . . . with blood and dirt" can indeed be a disturbing thought, and one we may be all too willing to forget. Against such knowledge it would seem the freshness of Cartesian doubt is nullified. However, Cartesian subjectivity has its uses and should not be discarded tout court. Necessary instead is to supplement it with another model of subjectivity that could continue to animate the learning process when the Cartesian model gets stonewalled. This model is provided by the "other side" of Cartesian philosophy, namely, psychoanalysis.[8]

III

Wo es war, soll ich werden—literally "Where it was, there I shall become."[9] This famous line of Freud's can be taken as his formula for the psychoanalytic subject. Where some alien knowledge once stood, the subjective *I* will come into being. It is almost a complete reversal of Descartes' "Cogito ergo sum." Whereas, in Descartes' line, subjectivity emerges when consciousness becomes emptied out of all content, leaving only the empty shell of thought itself, in Freud's, subjectivity emerges once the *I* absorbs or assumes a foreign body of knowledge. Freud's name for this foreign body of knowledge is none other than the unconscious.

With the concept of the unconscious, Freud is contending that individuals know more than they realize. The unconscious designates the form of knowledge that must remain repressed (in Freud, literally "sunken under" [*Verdrängung*]) if individuals are to conduct their activities undisturbed. In this way, the Cartesian cogito, in the Freudian view, actually becomes a defense against confronting the unconscious—that is, methodological doubt concerns itself with common knowledge precisely to avoid remembering repressed traumatic knowledge. Then, for

Freud, the conscious subject turns out to be not a subject at all. Because consciousness owes its uninterrupted existence to the constant repression of the unconscious, conscious subjects are in Freud's view automatons, systematically avoiding its disruptive signifiers.

As the unconscious troubles consciousness so thoroughly—as Freud's phrase "the return of the repressed" means to indicate—it is tempting to see psychoanalysis opposed to the philosophy of the subject. But, as we noted above, the point should not be to use psychoanalysis to reject Cartesian subjectivity: Freud is not against Descartes. The point, rather, is to find in the psychoanalytic doctrine of the unconscious the correlate for another side to subjectivity—namely, the subject of the unconscious.

Jacques Lacan made the Freud/Descartes comparison famous. The preferred reading of Lacan's work has been to see it as opposed to the Enlightenment doctrine of the subject—the so called decentering of the subject that became popular with poststructuralist theory.[10] Indeed Lacan himself claims his theory of the mirror-stage was meant to set psychoanalysis "at odds with any philosophy directly stemming from the *cogito*."[11] However, the preferred reading of Lacan's statement does not tell the whole story. By the time he gives his famous seminar on *The Four Fundamental Concepts of Psychoanalysis* it becomes decisively clear that Lacan's interest is in reviving the category of the subject, thus allying psychoanalysis with Enlightenment thought.[12] What Lacan is then opposed to is not Enlightenment thought but so-called ego-psychology, that is, the revisionist tradition that privileges the ego, making it the seat of subjectivity. We should thus read Lacan's statement "philosophy directly stemming from the *cogito*" not so much as singling out Descartes himself but as code for ego-psychology. "The important point," Lacan writes regarding the function of the mirror-stage, "is that this form situates the agency known as the ego, prior to its social determinations, in a fictional direction," and the ego "will only asymptotically approach the subject's becoming."[13]

Under the auspices of psychoanalysis, Lacan, however, salvages the subject by giving it entirely different grounds. Now, instead of grounding subjectivity on the ego, Lacan grounds subjectivity on the certainty of the unconscious. In psychoanalysis, the only thing we can be certain of is that the unconscious exists and that it thinks before consciousness can even reconcile it. The unconscious is therefore a subject. Thus, in Lacan's account, Freud does not reject Descartes but rather moves Descartes' project forward. Lacan states:

> In the term *subject* . . . I am not designating the living substratum needed by this phenomenon of the subject, nor any sort of substance, nor any being possessing knowledge in his *pathos*, his suffering . . . nor even some incarnated logos, but the Cartesian subject, who appears at the moment when doubt is recognized as certainty—except that, through my approach, the bases of this subject proves to be wider, but, at the same time much more amenable to the certainty that eludes it. This is what the unconscious is.
>
> (*S* XI:126, original emphasis)

As we can see, far from opposing Cartesian subjectivity, the psychoanalytic subject comes right out of it. Likewise, we must maintain that any attempt to reconstruct the student's subjective grounds is not a rejection of Freire's or Dewey's efforts but, rather, an attempt to push their respective projects forward.

IV

Let us now attend to Freud's discovery of the subject of the unconscious. Much of psychoanalysis, in both its theoretical apparatus and clinical application, comes out of a mapping of trauma, knowledge, and memory: what we know, how traumatic events affect that knowledge, and, subsequently, what we *choose* to forget. With Freud, it begins when he asks his patients to recount the etiological event of their symptoms. Of course, Freud's patients, as a rule, prove unable to remember anything. The memory of the traumatic event is effectively missing. Even in those fortunate cases where the missing memories could be supplied to Freud by a member of the patient's family or by the patient's physician, his patients nevertheless remain in their ignorance, avowing, all the while, to knowing nothing about the ancient causes of their illness, thus unable to corroborate those third-party sources. In the dossier entitled *Studies in Hysteria*,[14] Freud writes of the general characteristic of this so-called absent knowledge: "They were all of a distressing nature, fit to arouse the affects of shame, self-reproach, psychical pain and the feeling of impairment; all represented the kind of affect that one would like not to have experienced and would prefer to forget" (*Studies*, 270). "What resulted from this," Freud continues, "as if of its own accord, was the thought of *defence*" (original emphasis). What this means is that Freud did not simply consider the memories lost, his patients to be feebleminded, or the memories themselves to be unimpressive or inconsequential—the untenability of these trajectories is that they assume the patient is a passive actor in the forgetting. What Freud assumed is that the event that sets off the illness must be so traumatic that the mere recollection of the memory would be too painful to bear. Rather than being feebleminded, Freud thought his patients must be actively defending against this painful experience by claiming not to know anything about the original trauma. In those cases where Freud is supplied the crucial knowledge by an outside source, resistance is shown by the patients' insistence that they cannot corroborate those third-party accounts. Thus, the inability to remember is not passive forgetfulness but an active will to forget; Freud writes: "The hysteric's not-knowing was, therefore, a more or less conscious not-wanting-to-know, and the therapist's task," and this is the distinctive feature of psychoanalysis, "consists in overcoming the *resistance to association* through psychical work" (original emphasis).

So what Freud knows is this: first, his patients wish to avoid reexperiencing, via remembering, trauma; and second, they therefore resist learning knowledge associated with the original trauma by feeling the knowledge itself to be traumatic. But in what exact sense does trauma prevent recollection—that is to ask, what is the relationship between memory and trauma itself? The following answer suggests itself: the traumatic event is effectively and completely expunged from memory, any knowledge that is associated with it is felt as traumatic, and the patient therefore refuses to learn about this knowledge. Trauma, in this scenario, functions as an advanced warning, as a signal, that the knowledge one is being exposed to (or about to be exposed to) is unpleasant and therefore must not be allowed to be accepted by consciousness. Indeed a fairly straightforward hypothesis, but Freud suggests otherwise.

From his days of studying with Bernheim at his clinic in Nancy, Freud was well aware of the complexities involved in the function of memory. In *Studies in Hysteria*, Freud recalls, in particular, a demonstration performed by his teacher, Bernheim. In this demonstration Bernheim puts a woman into a hypnotic state and impresses upon her that he, Bernheim, is invisible to her; then, while the subject is in this somnambulistic state, Bernheim makes every effort to makes his presence known to her. After awakening her from her hypnotic state, Bernheim requests that she recall the events that just took place (i.e., everything he did to make her notice him, etc.), which she is, of course, unable to. "But he would not let it go at that," Freud tells us; Bernheim "claimed that she would remember everything, put his hand on her forehead so that she would think back and, lo and behold, she did finally relate everything that she claimed not to have perceived in her somnambulistic state and not have been cognizant of in her waking state" (113). What Bernheim's performance demonstrated was this: though she was not aware of it, the subject indeed possessed the knowledge he was seeking. The subject of Bernheim's demonstration exemplifies, in Freud words, a conscious "not-wanting-to-know."

Freud finds in this demonstration of Bernheim's the model of a technique he would carry with him when he fatefully decides to conduct his treatment of Miss Lucy R. without the aid of hypnosis. Freud's move is fateful, of course, insofar as it constitutes his break with hypnotic psychotherapy and the beginning of psychoanalysis proper; he writes: "I decided to work on the assumption that my patients knew everything that was of any pathogenic significance and that it was simply a question of making them communicate this." Borrowing from Bernheim, whenever a patient would claim to not know the answers to Freud's probes, Freud would count their claim as resistance and attempt to circumvent it with a *faux*-hypnotic gesture in which he, like Bernheim himself, would tell the patients that upon laying his hands on their forehead they would be able to recall the knowledge in question. The technique—which, to be sure, did not induce a somnambulistic state—proved extremely productive, to even Freud's own amazement.

Later, the Berheimian technique is sloughed off by Freud as psychoanalysis comes into its own, but the prototype met expectations as it clearly revealed that individuals possess knowledge laden with traumatic value, though they may not be consciously aware that they do. The knowledge is never completely expunged from memory—it leaves a residue. And when we feel unsettled by some material it is because it hits the traumatic knowledge we *always-already* possess. This, then, reverses the relationship between trauma and memory that we suggested in the above scenario. For trauma, in Freud's view, does not prevent the learning of difficult knowledge by forewarning us or by sending us discomforting signals; rather, it is an *effect*, a sign, that the traumatic knowledge we *always-already* possess is *once again* becoming conscious. Trauma, here, is still a signal—but a signal of a different kind. What it now signals is that we already possess some horrible knowledge and are actually recalling it. The resistance to learning exhibited by individuals is then a resistance toward *re*learning something that is on some level already imprinted in our memory. For this reason also, Freud intends the development of psychoanalytic technique to reach beyond the function of supplying the forgotten knowledge, which, no matter how obviously apropos the information might be, may simply be resisted. In this beyond, psychoanalytic technique now involves facilitating this process of relearning by putting the analysand to work at overcoming—that is, working through—their resistances.

A prime example of Freud's proposition on the relationship of trauma and memory can be found in another of his cases: the Ratman. The Ratman, an officer in the army, has a fateful meeting with the infamous "captain with a Czech name," of whom he relays: "I felt a certain fear of this man, *for he obviously took pleasure in cruelty*."[15] Already, the signs of trauma are apparent: visible in the Ratman's recollection is the uncanny sense that he already knows what a cruel man the Czech captain will turn out to be. On one occasion, this most cruel captain describes a certain kind of torture that he had read about involving the use of rats—hence, Freud's chosen pseudonym for his patient. The captain, true to form, takes immense enjoyment in describing the rat-punishment, and the horror caused by the sight of it sets Freud's patient off; specifically, it fills the Ratman with the compulsive obsession that harm might befall his loved ones. Yet, in the Ratman's case, trauma is a signal of what exactly? The trauma felt by the Ratman upon hearing the cruel captain's story throws him out of sorts not because it is a harbinger of darker things to come—though the Ratman might wish and insist it is. For Freud, attuned to the nuances of his patient's unconscious, the rat-punishment, as well as the captain himself, holds a traumatic resonance with his patient specifically because it evokes a knowledge the Ratman already possesses, namely, the knowledge that he desires to kill his father. Of course, the Ratman is incensed at Freud's interpretation and strongly affirms not knowing of such a desire. Thus the lesson of the Ratman: we always possess more knowledge than we would like to admit—sometimes more than we ourselves are consciously aware. Learning therefore does not always mean acquiring absolutely new knowledge; it sometimes requires relearning the traumatic knowledge we do "not-want-to-know" but possess all the same.

V

What Freud had discovered through his experimentation with pseudo-hypnotherapeutic techniques is nothing short of the theoretical innovation of psychoanalysis itself: namely, the unconscious. "We have learnt from psycho-analysis," Freud writes in his important essay on "The Unconscious," in the groundbreaking dossier *Papers on Metapsychology*, "that the essence of the process of repression lies, not in putting an end to, in annihilating, the idea which represents an instinct, but in preventing it from becoming conscious. When this happens we say of the idea that it is in a state of being 'unconscious'" (*SE* 14:166). Collected in the unconscious is a set or, in Lacan's terms, an entire discourse of repressed knowledge and not at all some forgotten emotion as is often believed. The unconscious, we might say, is the *form* taken by that knowledge we want to know nothing about—the underside of consciousness itself.

Lacan underscores the ideational rather than emotive character of the unconscious by formulating it thus: "The unconscious is the discourse of the Other."[16] In Lacan, the unconscious is articulated in advance in the symbolic order itself and speaks, in various ways, through the subject like an Other's discourse—for example, dreams, jokes, and the various psychopathologies of everyday life.[17]

Psychoanalysis never takes the position that the unconscious remains inaccessible to consciousness. Freud is abundantly clear on this point: "It is of course only as something conscious that we know it, after it has undergone transformation or translation into something conscious. Psycho-analytic work shows us every day that translation of this kind is possible." Freud continues: "In order that this [translation] should come about, the person under analysis must overcome certain resistances—the same resistances as those which, earlier, made the material concerned into something repressed by rejecting it from the conscious." If anything, the problem the unconscious presents is that it is ubiquitous; like an unwelcome houseguest, the unconscious is always imposing itself on consciousness and like a bone in our throats, goading us to reckon with it.[18] Freud, for example, tells the story of a man gravely ill whose doctor recommends he stay at a nursing home where they could surely "put an end to [*umbringen*]" him, then, quickly revises the parapraxes by stating he meant "take in [*unterbringen*]."[19] The slip of the doctor's tongue is, for Freud, more than a mere mistake; it reveals, rather, that the doctor knows, on an unconscious level, he will have to euthanize the man. The doctor himself is unaware of what his unconscious knows as he quickly corrects himself and assures the ill man that he simply misspoke. The problem for the doctor is that the unconscious forced its way into his conscious speech—not at all that it evades his grasp. Thus, for psychoanalysis, it is the subject who is culpable for missing the encounters with the unconscious, not the unconscious itself.

VI

The psychoanalytic notion of knowledge articulated in advance in the form of the symbolic order—that is, the discourse of the Other—finds its Marxian concomitant in the theory of class consciousness proposed by Georg Lukacs.[20] Criticisms of the Marxian concept of class consciousness often follow two tracks: either (a) class consciousness posits the contents of what individuals of a certain social group are "supposed" to think at the cost of implying that their actually existing thoughts are illegitimate, irrelevant, erroneous—in short, so-called false consciousness, or (b) the moment of class consciousness has the feeling of a "Great Awakening," of the Marxian variety, in which individuals miraculously pierce the "veil of ideology." If anything, Lukacs—the premiere expositor of the concept of class consciousness—would do nothing but *agree* with these objections. For Lukacs defends a radically different conception of class consciousness; he writes: "Now class consciousness consists in fact of the appropriate and rational reactions 'imputed' to a particular typical position in the process of production" (*History*, 51). Note how Lukacs argues class consciousness is a structural feature of the production process, not a personal one. He goes on: "This consciousness is, therefore, neither the sum nor the average of what is thought or felt by the single individuals who make up the class," and he continues, "This analysis establishes right from the start the distance that separates class consciousness from the empirically given, and from the psychologically describable and explicable ideas which men form about their situation in life" (51). Again, note how Lukacs posits a distance or gap between the content of class consciousness and the thoughts of actual empirical people. For Lukacs, class consciousness is a set of knowledge that somehow exists objectively without making claims of correctness on the thoughts of individuals.

Class consciousness is thus the knowledge of the mode of production contained, or as Lukacs has it, "imputed," to a particular structural class position within the total system; its thrust is that it places knowledge on the side of the system itself. It no longer much matters what individuals actually think or know about the system. The system functions regardless; and by functioning, the system literally "thinks" the appropriate thoughts for individuals. For example, the individual worker need not imagine extracting living labor power from the body in order to sell it as a commodity on the market in order for capitalism to function. This knowledge—that is, of classes and their particular functions—is possessed by the system of capital production itself, and as it operates, the system literally thinks about the extraction, sale, and consumption of labor power so that the individual does not have to. In other words, while empirical individuals may not care about the economy or politics, the economy and politics care about empirical individuals. Class consciousness, in other words, on Lukacs's account, exists on a similar formal level as does the psychoanalytic unconscious.

To get a better flavor for what Lukacs means by the "rational reactions 'imputed' to a particular typical position in the process of production," we need only turn to Marx himself. Explaining the rationale for his presentation in *Capital*, Marx writes this in the "Preface to the First Edition":

> I do not by any means depict the capitalist and the landowner in rosy colours. But individuals are dealt with here only in so far as they are the personifications of economic categories, the bearers of particular class-relations and interests. My standpoint,

from which the development of the economic formation of
society is viewed as a process of natural history, can less than
any other make the individual responsible for relations whose
creature he remains, socially speaking, however much he may
subjectively raise himself above them.

(*Capital*, 92)

Marx's claim is that, in *Capital*, he sets out to describe and
analyze the metaphysical system called capitalism, not to give an
ethnographic account of life in a capitalist society. Thus Marx
warns that the individuals who appear in the work should not
be read as references to empirical individuals. They are instead,
as Marx himself puts it, "personifications" of class positions.
The upshot is that the particular actions Marx describes individuals performing are, in actuality, the structural functions
imputed to the class positions themselves. This is why Marx
clarifies that he can only hold individuals accountable according to the actions capitalism organizes for their class and not
according to the actions an empirical individual may actually
perform, which might sometimes go against the grain of their
class position. These actions capitalism requires the respective
classes to perform—in Marx's terms, the personifications of
the class positions—are what Lukacs dubs consciousness. What
"the personification of economic categories (i.e., class)" is to
Marx, "the rational reactions 'imputed' to a particular typical
position in the process of production (i.e., class consciousness)"
is to Lukacs.

The obvious strength of the Lukacsian conception of class
consciousness is how it elegantly refutes the two criticisms
mentioned above. First, "false consciousness" has nothing to do
with the status of individuals' thoughts and, especially, nothing whatsoever to do with the distance that may separate what
people think from what they "should" think—however "should"
is determined. What makes a consciousness false is the associated
structural position itself: "Thus the barrier which converts the
class consciousness of the bourgeoisie into 'false' consciousness
is objective; it is the class situation itself. It is the objective result

of the economic set-up, and is neither arbitrary, subjective nor psychological" (*History*, 54). False consciousness does not, for Lukacs, refer to the distance separating individuals' thoughts and the knowledge ascribed to their class position; rather, false consciousness refers to the consciousness of the bourgeois class itself. The bourgeois class position simply does not proffer a standpoint wide enough to glimpse all sides of the mode of production and therefore its consciousness is inherently false.

As for the criticism of class consciousness having the scent of religion: unlike in religion, where religious consciousness is attained through a religious experience, class consciousness, for Lukacs, can be attained despite not having experienced a particular class position—or class standpoint, as he calls it. Rather, standpoints are available as methodological vistas for viewing the social totality. Therefore, there is no moment, episode, or experience at which we "see the light." It is simply a matter of which standpoint we take when examining the system. A matter of which position we decide to become the subject. In the place of religious metaphors, we now find scientific or perspectival ones. In advancing this nonessentialist theory of class standpoints, Lukacs merely echoes Marx when the latter writes: "A class . . . from which emanates the consciousness of the necessity of a fundamental revolution, the communist consciousness, which may, of course, arise among the other classes too through the contemplation of the situation of this class."[21]

But as suggestive and provocative Lukacs's unadulterated Marxian variation on consciousness may be, even he does not take into account the various resistances, in the psychoanalytic sense of the word, individuals will produce in order not to know the traumatic knowledge yielded by certain standpoints. We must therefore follow through with the formal characterization of class consciousness as the unconscious and suggest that the problem proletariat class consciousness presents an individual is that it is always intruding into the individual's peaceful outlook, thus inducing various resistances on the part of the individual subject. We cannot thus "merely" occupy a standpoint; rather, such an act itself involves rigor and work, specifically, the work of overcoming resistances to it.

VII

Just as Lukacs correlates class consciousness to the system itself, effectively rubbing out the individual's relevance, so Lacan and psychoanalysis also correlate the unconscious to a kind of nonindividual subject: "If there is an image which could represent for us the Freudian notion of the unconscious, it is indeed that of the acephalic subject, of a subject who no longer has an ego, who doesn't belong to the ego" (*S* II:167). Lacan describes his notion of the subject as acephalic (that is, headless) because its thought is no longer tied to the consciousness of the ego but is now taken over by the unconscious itself. Because of its ties to the ego, consciousness is considered by Lacan as an obstacle or resistance to the knowledge of the unconscious. In dividing thought and being between the unconscious and the subject, Lacan introduces a fundamental division into his variation on the subject, that is to say, the Lacanian subject is a split-subject, which he conveys in his nomenclature: $. Lukacs, similarly, introduces a split into the subject of the proletariat with class consciousness, as we saw, on the side of the system itself, separated from the individual's being. In both Lukacs and Lacan, the acephalic subject becomes the image to which we must hold on.

The overcoming of the ego leaves a clearing in which the subject of the unconscious can emerge. This is why, for Lacan, the subject can only be described negatively. Only when conscious thought or positive identity (i.e., I am a man, I am a teacher, I am able-bodied, etc.)—in short, the ego—is subtracted from individuals, that is, only when they are transformed into the negativity that is the Lacanian subject, can they learn the unconscious.

Having established the primacy of the unconscious in psychoanalytic thought, its relation to subjectivity, and the affinity between the psychoanalytic unconscious and the Marxian conception of class consciousness, what is now wanted is an account of the exact processes or mechanisms through which an individual passes from ego-consciousness to the subject of the unconscious. Before turning to Lacan for this schema in a moment, let us complete the discussion on trauma. If class consciousness corresponds to the unconscious in that they are both forms of repressed knowledge, then trauma would be the sign of class consciousness's emergence. Therefore the criticism that Marx issues his political economist contemporaries on the basis of their not having learned the miserable truth of capitalist accumulation is a bit off the mark. For Marx grants them too much benefit of the doubt. More correct would have been to make the psychoanalytic critique, namely, that the bourgeois political economists knew this truth quite well but nonetheless did "not want to know" about it. They felt the trauma of capitalism and attempted to rationalize it away.

VIII

In Lacan's account, subject formation begins with his theory of the mirror-stage.[22] The theory begins appropriately with a child in front of a mirror. At this crucial moment, the child is still at a developmental stage in which it has yet to master various bodily parts and functions. Able neither to fend for itself nor to stand on its own power, nor even to exhibit control over its bowels, the child is still experiencing itself as a fragmented confederation rather than as a unified system. What the child receives from the mirror is the first image of itself as a coherent whole, an overall gestalt, an "'orthopedic' form of its totality" ("Mirror Stage," 6). The child recognizes its reflection as itself and forms a relationship of identification with it, that is, a relationship based on sameness—to paraphrase, the child thinks of its image thus: "The reflection is me, and *I* am that reflection;" hence, the formation of the *I*-function. In Lacan's words, the child literally *occupies* the position of its mirror-image. Precipitated from this encounter is, of course, the ego: "The jubilant assumption of his specular image . . . thus seems to me to manifest in an exemplary situation the symbolic matrix in which the *I* is precipitated in a primordial form" (4).

Some years after presenting the version of the "Mirror Stage" essay we have in the famous *Écrits*, Lacan states the following in his seminar on *Freud's Papers on Technique*: "You know that the process of his physiological maturation allows the subject, at a moment in his history, to integrate effectively his motor functions, and to gain access to a real mastery of his body. Except the subject becomes aware of his body as a totality prior to this particular moment"(*S* I:79). These comments set up the mirror-stage theory's full significance, which Lacan states this way: "That is what I insist upon in my theory of the mirror-stage— the sight alone of the whole form of the human body gives the subject an imaginary mastery over his body, one which is premature in relation to a real mastery" (79). Thus, for Lacan, seeing an image of itself as a totality does more than endow the child with a false sense of wholeness, it also gives the child a sense of self-mastery. As the child moves, so does its reflection. This mimetic response gives the child the feeling that it animates and therefore controls its image. But unlike the "anal stage" Freud formulates, which designates the stage where the child begins to master itself in the real by first controlling its own bowel movements, the Lacanian mirror-stage offers an imaginary self-mastery that anticipates any real experience. The mirror-stage thus represents a quantum leap in development: the child goes from not having any control over its own body directly to possessing an absolute yet imaginary mastery of itself.

The significance of Lacan's elucidation is this: what the child recognizes— or, more accurately put, *mis*recognizes—in the mirror is not its real fleshly body as an ordered physiological system but, rather, a specular self, a semblance, or, in more technical terms, an *imago*. What this means for the ego is that it is grounded upon identification with an idealized and imaginary version of the self—that is, as a totality—and not at all on anything concrete. This is why the ego's fate is to turn out to be something very fragile—susceptible to psychotic dissolution, targeted by neurotic attacks, objectified in fantasy-life, and so on—being precariously sustained by subsequent identifications with other *imagoes*.

Though Lacan uses unflattering terms like "misrecognition" and "imaginary" in describing the ego and the mirror-relation, his point is not to argue the obsolescence of these functions. The imaginary should not be understood as being nonexistent, make believe, or something of that sort; rather, it should be seen as one register in Lacan's tripartite model of reality ("the symbolic"—language, codes, culture, etc.—and "the real"—materiality itself—being the other two). The imaginary, moreover, provides the individual with a connection to the real; he writes: "The function of the mirror stage thus turns out, in my view, to be a particular case of the function of imagos, which is to establish a relationship between an organism and its reality" ("Mirror Stage," 6). He also states: "This [the mirror-stage] is the original adventure through which man, for the first time, has the experience of seeing himself, of reflecting on himself and conceiving of himself as other than he is—an essential dimension of the human, which entirely structures his fantasy life" (*S* I:79). Lacan's critique of the ego is aimed at undoing the aggrandizement it receives at the hands of ego-psychology. Nor does Lacan conceive the mirror to be duping the child into identifying with its reflection, even going as far as to describe the mirror-relation as a genuine "act of intelligence" ("Mirror Stage," 3). As far as its identification function is concerned: the mirror-stage is the primary identification, as Lacan calls it, "the rootstock," for further secondary identifications with other imagoes—whether these imagoes exude from within as self-idealizations (the ideal-ego) or come from without in the form of others we take as our models (the ego-ideal).

As we can see, Lacan's intention is to put the imaginary register back in its place and not at all to do away with it. What is at stake in Lacan's corrective is subjectivity itself: for Lacan, only the unconscious, and not the ego, can serve as the basis of the psychoanalytic subject. Ego-consciousness—referred to here as the *I* function—exists in the imaginary register is and moreover grounded on a primary misrecognition of and identification with a semblance of wholeness. As such, to aggrandize the ego by making it synonymous with subjectivity is indeed to base one's faith on a foundation of sand. In Lacan, it is precisely the ego that must be stripped away in order to make room for the subject of the unconscious. What he theorizes as necessary is then a separation with the mirror-image, to gain a distance from the ego by deidentifying with it.

IX

As Lacan's work progresses, so too does his thoughts on the mirror-stage. In the later years, he begins to devote much of his energies precisely to the issue of separation. And by the time of his seminar *Encore*, Lacan is able to conceptualize the separation process by emphasizing that the mirror (as with any discursive field) always contains a point where sense dissipates and disruption begins—where knowledge, as he puts it, "doesn't stop not being written" (*S* XX:94).

Lacan designates this nonsensical object in the mirror-field, the object *a*—a kernel of nonsense that escapes symbolization and is thus unassumable.[23] Unable to occupy or identify with the object *a* within its reflection, the child's reflection is rendered unrecognizable and the identification process is thereby interrupted. Of course, the child can construct a fiction in order to reconcile or rationalize the object *a* rather than be separated from the ego. This fiction is what is known in psychoanalysis as the fundamental fantasy. Lacan's formula for fantasy is: $\$<>a$—which is meant to show how the individual must close the gap the object *a* opens up by projecting a narrative fantasy that can account for its presence.[24] But in the gap the object *a* temporarily opens up, a space is cleared for the subject of the unconscious to emerge.

We find a fine illustration of this disruptive process of separation enabling subjectivity in a mirror-experience Freud himself recalls in his essay "The Uncanny."[25] In the final footnote to that essay, Freud recalls a train ride in which a jolt opens the door in his compartment. At that moment Freud sees a man in the doorway who he supposes entered his compartment by mistake. "I jumped up to put him right," Freud recounts, "but soon realized to my astonishment that the intruder was my own image, reflected in the mirror on the connecting door. I can still recall that I found his appearance thoroughly unpleasant" (162). Uncanny is how Freud describes the experience of failed recognition, and it is an exemplary description of the object *a*'s disruptive function. Thus Lacanian theory would account for this experience of failed recognition—Freud's uncanny—this way: within the mirror is a place where knowledge "doesn't stop not being written," and it is this "uncanny object" that disrupts Freud's ability to recognize his own image thereby effectively separating Freud from his own ego-image. There in that split-moment of nonrecognition—in the uncanny itself—emerges the psychoanalytic subject.[26]

In the moment of separation and nonrecognition, the ego is truncated and consciousness's head is cut off—the subject is made acephalic. Devoid of an ego to defend against the unconscious, the individual catches up to the knowledge that the unconscious contains—that is to say, a unity is made between the individual's being and the knowledge of the unconscious. Thus with Lacan, Descartes' formula for subjectivity—the famous cogito ergo sum—is preserved, but preserved by its reversal and inversion: "I am thinking where I am not, therefore I am where I am not thinking."[27]

X

According to a psycho-Marxian matrix, we cannot assume that a social investigator can access society's dark underside and learn its traumatic knowledge without showing any resistance. In fact, the psychoanalytic claim is far more radical: the social investigator, in some sense, already knows the terrible truth and is in fact trying to repress it. When it comes to traumatic knowledge, learning never proceeds progressively from a zero level to full knowledge. The problem presented by traumatic knowledge is that it always-already exists in advance of the subject's being. For Marxism, this means one cannot conceptualize the problematic of class consciousness to be solely the problem of exposing people to class standpoints that yield the knowledge of exploitation and oppression. What is needed in addition is a way of dealing with resistances—more precisely, with the individual's ego that defends against occupying class standpoints.

For the learning process to take place, then a negative gesture is needed—that is, a striking away of all egotistical investments that prevent us from real (as opposed to imaginary) learning. Above we called this negative moment "failed recognition" or "separation." In the space opened up by this clearing away emerges a kind of subject to correspond with class consciousness. In other words, class consciousness, in the Lukacian sense, is like the unconscious in that it is articulated in advance in the system itself. Yet, we are prevented from learning class consciousness by our own resistances to the standpoints that lead to it. When a moment of failed recognition occurs—that is, when a correspondence between our subjective, self-rendered, image of ourselves and our objective position in the mode of production is ruptured—we are able to occupy the necessary standpoints for class consciousness.

To complete the articulation of Lacan with Lukacs or psychoanalysis with Marxism, we must find a social embodiment for the disruptive kernel of object *a*. But what is the object *a*—that point of nonsense that our rational consciousness cannot comprehend—if not a version of what Marxism calls "contradiction"? After all, is contradiction not that point where the system comes into conflict with itself thereby undermining its own circuitry from within? Were not the contradictions of capitalism the very things that remained incomprehensible to the bourgeois political economists, from Smith and Ricardo, through Locke and Mill, to the present? And instead of recognizing contradictions as the points where knowledge "doesn't stop not being written," did bourgeois political economy not produce so many fictional fantasies to explain them away? In that case, we can see Marx's critical contribution to political economy as an ethical unwillingness to cover over the contradictions of capitalism and to accept instead the separation with his subjective identity precipitated therewith.

Confronted with contradictions, the social investigator should make no attempt to rationalize them away and should instead conceive of them as integral features of the system itself. The negative space left by the refusal to assimilate one's self to the system (i.e., identify with it) opens up the possibility for one to become the subject of traumatic knowledge. We might call this void the psychoanalytic or Lacanian subject or the proletariat subject with equal accuracy. But, perhaps, most apropos would be to call it simply this: the student.

Wo es war, soll ich werden—Where it was, there I shall become.

5

Pedagogy of the Repressed: Repetition As a Pedagogical Factor

I

Critical pedagogy, as far as I understand it, is the project of making learners conscious of their social conditions.[1] Often, various forms of oppression and social injustice make these conditions problematic. Advocates of critical pedagogy have traditionally emphasized oppression along class lines and more recently have acknowledged its manifestation along racial, ethnic, national, gender, and sexual lines as well. The key figure in the development of critical pedagogy is, of course, Paulo Freire.[2] Freire argues that the pedagogical relationship does not exist outside of the broader social relations that critical pedagogy wants to make conscious. That is to say, if those social conditions are oppressive, then the pedagogical relationship reflects that oppressiveness at least in part. Making those oppressive conditions conscious thus requires a different kind of pedagogical relationship than what already exists. Critical pedagogy must offer that different pedagogical relationship. This new pedagogical relationship, as Freire has it, is predicated upon dialogue. "To be an act of knowing," he writes, "the adult literacy process demands among teachers and students a relationship of authentic dialogue."[3] "True dialogue unites subjects together in the cognition of a knowable object that mediates between them."

In 1989, Elizabeth Ellsworth's provocative and probing essay "Why Doesn't This Feel Empowering"[4] appeared in print. In this essay, Ellsworth asked serious questions of critical pedagogy and took many of its assumptions to task. Ellsworth recounts a course she taught, "Media and Anti-Racist Pedagogies" ("Why," 299), in which critical pedagogy was used as the framework. What she finds is that the practice of critical pedagogy is ineffectual for achieving its own stated goals. The problem, she argues, is a rhetoric that operates at a "high level of abstraction," (300) which is more "appropriate (yet hardly more helpful) for philosophical debates," and ultimately "offers only the most abstract, decontextualized criteria for choosing one position over others" (300–301). The problem with critical pedagogy's rhetoric is that a number of assumptions remain hidden behind abstractions. For example, in setting up dialogue as the new, more freeing, pedagogical relationship, an "irrational Other" (301) is assumed to exist while the rational dialogic subject assumes qualities that are constitutive of a "European, White, male, middle class, Christian, able-bodied, thin, and heterosexual" (304) subject. In projecting these assumed qualities as embodying an antioppressive ideal, silence is posited as that irrational— ultimately, oppressed—Other instead of being grasped as a "highly complex negotiation of the politics of knowing and being known" (313). In forcing students into dialogue, critical pedagogy forces students to participate in "the logics of rationalism and scientism which have been predicated on and made possible through the exclusion of socially constructed irrational Others—women, people of color, nature, aesthetics" (305):

> As Audre Lorde writes, "The master's tools will never dismantle the master's house," and to call on students of color to justify and explicate their claims in terms of the master's tools—tools such as rationalism, fashioned precisely to perpetuate their exclusion—colludes with the oppressor in keeping "the oppressed occupied with the master's concerns."

In other words, critical pedagogy, for Ellsworth, relies upon "repressive myths that perpetuate relations of domination" (298).

Ellsworth's analysis is incisive, her critiques are devastating, and her rhetoric is strong. Indeed, her essay touched off a bit of a firestorm, with academics, all over, taking sides.[5] I have no interest in either revisiting these debates or taking sides. However, I do want to note that the strong reaction was unfortunate since, as far as I see it, Ellsworth and her interlocutors share the same goal of achieving social justice. Moreover, the reaction is particularly odd since the central thrust of Ellsworth's argument was already anticipated by Freire himself. Freire writes, in his most foundational text, *Pedagogy of the Oppressed*: "But almost always, during the initial stage of the struggle, the oppressed, instead of striving for liberation, tend themselves to become oppressors, or 'sub-oppressors'" (*Oppressed*, 45). The reason there is this regression is that the "very structure of their thought has been conditioned by the concrete, existential situation by which they were shaped." That "existential situation" is one in which the oppressor serves as the model of humanity. Thus, for the oppressed, "to be men is to be oppressors."

Because of this contradiction, Freire argues, overcoming oppression cannot occur immediately but only after the oppressed "first critically recognize its causes" (47)—a recognition that is achieved through pedagogy. This "pedagogy of the oppressed" is one that "makes oppression and its causes objects of reflection by the oppressed" (48). This pedagogy is predicated upon dialogue. But this dialogue is itself formed within that same social context or "existential situation," and it, as a result, Ellsworth points out, exhibits similar oppressive traits as those found in the context itself. Moreover, Freire's claim about the oppressed becoming oppressors applies to the so-called liberators and their pedagogy: the liberator, during the initial stage of the struggle, instead of striving to liberate, tends to become an oppressor.

Nothing thus far should be surprising. The real question is how a pedagogy that reflects some of the oppressive qualities of the social situation will achieve the goal of making conscious the causes of oppression. Freire, as far as I read him, never clearly works out how dialogue overcomes its own contradictions, but he does nevertheless leave enough clues to allow us to speculate as to what that answer might be.

The first clue is Freire's analysis of the oppressed's tendency to become themselves oppressors: "At this level, their perception of themselves as opposites of the oppressor does not yet signify engagement in a struggle to overcome the contradiction; the one pole aspires not to liberation, but to identification with its opposite pole" (45–46). Note that Freire formulates the problem in psychoanalytic terms: namely, he calls it, *identification*. The use of psychoanalytic concepts is curious given that Freire never explicitly references Freud or Lacan.[6] But while he never mentions those names, Freire repeatedly refers to Albert Memmi, Franz Fanon, Herbert Marcuse, Eric Fromm, and Louis Althusser—all of whom were well versed in Freudian and/or Lacanian psychoanalytic theory. The recourse to these psychoanalytic thinkers is the second clue. The third clue comes with Freire's description of the "type of false perception" (52) that "occurs when a change in objective reality would threaten the individual or class interests of the perceiver."

> In the first instance, there is no critical intervention in reality because that reality is fictitious; there is none in the second instance because intervention would contradict the class interests of the perceiver. In the latter case the tendency of the perceiver is to behave "neurotically." The fact exists; but both the fact and what may result from it may be prejudicial to the person. Thus it becomes necessary, not precisely to deny the fact, but to "see it differently." This rationalization as a defense mechanism coincides in the end with subjectivism.

Freire's use of psychoanalytic language ("neurotically," "rationalization," and "defense mechanism") is undeniable. The fourth and decisive clue comes on the heels of observing that the oppressor will often act generously toward the oppressed: "Discovering himself to be an oppressor may cause considerable anguish, but it does not necessarily lead to solidarity with the oppressed. Rationalizing his guilt through paternalistic treatment of the oppressed, all the while holding them fast in a position of dependence, will not do" (49). Freire then suggests that psycho-analysis is necessary to understand this paternalistic generosity: "A psychoanalysis of oppressive action might reveal the false generosity of the oppressor . . . as a dimension of the latter's sense of guilt" (146). Unfortunately for us, Freire never conducts this "psychoanalysis of oppressive action," but his acknowledge-ment of psychoanalytic insight is enough to warrant further investigation. If psychoanalytic concepts are needed to better understand the problems of social oppression and the struggle to become more human, then psychoanalysis, I claim, is needed to formulate answers.[7] In this chapter, I will offer some provisional answers by way of the psychoanalytic concept of repetition.

II

In his claim that the mindset of the oppressed is conditioned by their "existential situation," Freire grasps perfectly Lacan's claim that "the unconscious is the discourse of the Other."[8] Lacan explains: "Now, the discourse of the Other that is to be realized, that of the unconscious, is not beyond the closure, it is *outside*" (*S* XI:131, original emphasis). Outside: that is how Lacan describes the location of the unconscious. What could he possibly mean? The "Other," for Lacan, is, in the first place, not an individual person but the "site of the pure subject of the signifier."[9] In other words, the Other is the field of social relations, the symbolic order, or discourse insofar as discourse is, for Lacan, supralinguistic:

> I designate it with the term "discourse" because there's no other way to designate it once we realize that the social link is instated only by anchoring itself in the way in which language is situated over and etched into what the place is crawling with, namely, speaking beings.
>
> (*S* XX:54)

The Other, that is to say, designates the field in which individuals are socially linked. This social field that comprises the Other is, for Lacan, the unconscious. The unconscious is not an emotional core that is deeply embedded within the brain but rather the field of discourse that governs and determines how individuals relate to each other and to even themselves. To understand the unconscious, one must not look inwardly but outwardly to the field of social relations. To observe the structures of society is to observe the unconscious.

Slavoj Zizek helpfully comments that Lacan's thesis that "the unconscious is the discourse of the Other" designates a "form of thought whose ontological status is not that of thought, that is to say, the form of thought external to the thought itself."[10] The unconscious is "some Other scene external to thought" (19)—insofar as the "Lacanian 'big Other' does not designate merely the explicit symbolic rules regulating social interactions, but also the intricate cobweb of 'unwritten' rules"[11]—"whereby the form of thought is already articulated in advance" (*Sublime Object*, 19). Zizek turns to Pascal's notion of belief to exemplify Lacan's logic. According to Zizek, Pascal thinks belief does not reside in the mind but in the body's participation in religious rituals such that the body is "the automaton, which leads the mind unconsciously along with it" (cited in *Sublime Object*, 36). "By following a custom," Zizek explains, "the subject believes without knowing it, so that the final conversion is merely a formal act by means of which we recognize what we have already believed" (40). But Zizek warns against understanding Pascal as advancing a behaviorist notion of belief as if belief were the outcome of being socialized into a religious order. More to the point, if, for Pascal, we believe when we participate in rituals, it is because "our belief is," literally "already materialized in the external ritual" (43) itself. Zizek writes: "The lesson to be drawn from this concerning the social field is above all that belief, far from being an 'intimate,' purely mental state, is always *materialized* in our effective social activity" (36, original emphasis). Pascalian belief exemplifies the unconscious in the way it exists outside the mind in the form of ritual itself. On this account, "the unconscious is not a kind of transcendent, unattainable thing of which we are unable to take cognizance, it is rather . . . an overlooking: we overlook the way our act is already part of the state of things we are looking at" (59). Or, to put it another way, the unconscious is thought externalized so that we can see what is going on "inside" by looking outside.

Thus, rather than thinking of the unconscious as some emotional core that is tucked away within the individual subject's mind, Lacan would have us think of it as the field of social relations that constitutes the milieu in which the subject exists materially. The unconscious exists, as Lacan puts it, "outside" the subject. The unconscious conditions the subject—a process usually called introjection or internalization—and makes itself known by speaking through the subject like some other's discourse. Freire records this operation, within the context of Memmi's "colonized mentality" no less: "Self-depreciation is another characteristic of the oppressed, which derives from their internalization of the opinion the oppressors hold of them. So often do they hear that they are good for nothing, know nothing and are incapable of learning anything . . . that in the end they become convinced of their own unfitness" (*Oppressed*, 63). Up to this point, Freire uses a concept of the unconscious (borrowed from Memmi), but it is not necessarily Lacanian. Then, Freire recounts: "Not infrequently, peasants in educational projects begin to discuss a generative theme in a lively manner, then stop suddenly and say to the educator: 'Excuse us, we ought to keep quiet and let you talk. You are the one who knows, we don't know anything'" (63). The unconscious social conditions speak through the oppressed: the oppressed are literally automatic mouthpieces through which oppressive society announces itself as *I* like some other's discourse. The way oppressive social conditions are not simply internalized but actually speak through the voices of the oppressed draws upon a distinctly Lacanian conception of the unconscious.

III

"As long as the oppressed remain unaware of the causes of their condition," Freire writes, "they fatalistically 'accept' their exploitation" (64). That process of "raising awareness" involves learning the knowledge of the unconscious. Lacan's concept of the unconscious means, however, that learning will not be a process of personal introspection (self-reflection is distinctly Freirean) but of external examination, of grasping the social factors that condition one's existential position, which voice themselves through one's speech.

Learning the unconscious is, of course, never easy. If it encounters much resistance, it is not because the unconscious is inscrutable but, much rather, because it is repressed. Repression means that the unconscious is never completely obliterated or expunged; rather, "the essence of repression lies simply in turning something away, and keeping it at a distance, from the conscious."[12] Or, to put it another way, repression is a form of intentional forgetting. "Forgetting impressions, scenes or experiences," as Freud reminds us, "nearly always reduces itself to shutting them off," so that, "when the patient talks about these 'forgotten' things," they really mean, "as a matter of fact I've always known it; only I've never thought of it" (*SE* 12:148). Since forgetting is only an appearance, Freud describes the psychoanalytic learning process thus: "Descriptively speaking, it is to fill in gaps in memory; dynamically speaking, it is to overcome resistances due to repression." Learning what is unconscious can be better described as a process of remembering or relearning, not a learning for the first time.

In the psychoanalytic situation, the unconscious is remembered in two ways. The first way of remembering is the rather straightforward process of becoming conscious of supposedly forgotten knowledge. Here, the subject is simply made aware of the unconscious, which then becomes the topic of conversation. Focused on "raising awareness," Freire takes into account only this, first, way of remembering, as is clearly seen in his offered example:

> It is striking, however, to observe how this self-depreciation changes with the first changes in the situation of oppression. I heard a peasant leader say in an *asentamiento* meeting, "They used to say we were unproductive because we were lazy and drunkards. All lies. Now that we are respected as meant, we're

going to show everyone that we were never drunkards or lazy. We were exploited!"

(*Oppressed*, 64)

In this excerpt, Freire recollects a moment when the oppressed became cognizant of the oppressive social structures that lie in the unconscious.

The conscious form of remembering is obviously a powerful way of achieving the goals of critical pedagogy. But psycho-analysis theorizes a second method of remembering that must be taken into account as a pedagogical factor: "We may say that the patient does not *remember* anything of what he has forgotten and repressed, but *acts* it out" (*SE* 12:150, original emphasis). In acting out, the patient "reproduces it not as a memory but as an action; he *repeats* it, without, of course, knowing that he is repeating it" (150, original emphasis). Acting out, or *repetition,* is, for Freud, a way of remembering: "As long as the patient is in the treatment he cannot escape from this compulsion to repeat; and in the end we understand that this is his way of remembering." For example, "the patient does not say that he remembers that he used to be defiant and critical towards his parents' authority; instead, he behaves in that way to the doctor."

The main difference between these two forms is that repetition is an unconscious act of remembering. The memory is brought within the context of the analysis but in such a way that it eludes consciousness. Because it is a remembering that keeps its contents away from the conscious, repetition is also a form of resistance: "The greater the resistance, the more exten-sively will acting out (repetition) replace remembering" (151). The conscious form of remembering is, of course, ideal; but it only takes place when "resistance has been put completely on one side." Resistance is weakest when a positive rapport—what Freud calls, positive transference—exists between the analyst and analysand. Those ideal conditions are never always the case, and as "the transference becomes hostile or unduly intense and therefore in need of repression, remembering at once gives way to acting out." "It is, of course, only as something conscious that we know it" (*SE* 14:166), as Freud reminds us, which is why psychoanalysis focuses attention on the memory function of repetition and "celebrates it as a triumph for the treatment if [the analyst] can bring it about that something that the patient wishes to discharge in action is disposed of through the work of remembering" (*SE* 12:153). Repetition has, in other words, the potential to become conscious.

What is remembered by repetition is the same as what is (potentially) remembered by the conscious: namely, "everything that has already made its way from the sources of the repressed into his manifest personality—his inhibitions and unservice-able attitudes and his pathological character-traits" (151). In Freirean terms, what gets repeated and thus remembered in the beginning stages of struggle are the oppressive conditions themselves, and this is why it always appears that the oppressed and the liberators both want to become themselves oppres-sors: oppression is being repeated. However, repetition has a distinct and decisive advantage over the conscious: whereas the conscious stages memories as past events, repetition presents them as a "piece of real life" (152), thus allowing them to be confronted as a "present-day force" (151). Of course, repetition is a very complicated form of remembering, and, if not handled properly, it can run amok of the situation, especially since it is also a resistance. But because of its ability to make memories felt in the present, it represents a superior form of remembering. In terms of critical pedagogy, repetition allows social categories, which are often seen, as Ellsworth points out, almost only as abstractions, to be felt as a lived realities. The oppressed not only know oppression but can see it played out in real time through its repetition in the classroom. Liberating educators can use coercive techniques or guilt to make students see things their way, for example. Or, oppressed students can strive to curry favor with the educator by putting down other students. These are just a few examples of how oppressive structures are remembered by repetition in the classroom.

Returning to Ellsworth's account of the disempowering results of critical pedagogy, if I may—one way of thinking about the disempowering relations that were played out in the classroom might be to see them as being remembered through their repetition. It might be the case that all those "repressive myths," uncovered by Ellsworth, exist within critical pedagogy's dialogic method because it is a method that allows for repetition to take place. If we remain closed off to the memory process of repetition, then critical pedagogy simply appears to be itself an oppressive pedagogy. But if repetition is taken into account—and this is why, I argue, it must be seen as a pedagogical factor—then critical pedagogy becomes an excellent method for allowing oppression to move from the level of abstract knowledge down to the level of lived experience. Repetition is what makes critical pedagogy more effective than, say, a traditional lecture about sexism or racism—repetition makes it a "present-day force." The point is not to prevent repetition; rather, it is to work out and work through repetition so that it can become known to consciousness—critical pedagogy must become psychopedagogy.

IV

Freud notes that patients often begin analysis with repetition: "Above all, the patient will *begin* his treatment with a repetition of this kind" (150, original emphasis). This inaugural repetition often appears in the form of transference toward the analyst: "We soon perceive that the transference is itself only a piece of repetition, and that the repetition is a transference of the forgotten past not only on to the doctor but also on to all the other aspects of the current situation" (151). Freire, speaking about his educational projects, observes something very similar to this inaugural repetition. In *Pedagogy of Hope*, he recounts a conversation with Chilean workers: "We began a lively dialogue, with questions and replies on both sides—promptly followed, however, by a disconcerting silence."[13] Freire had encountered this "disconcerting silence" many times before in his work in Brazil:

> I too remained silent. In the silence, I remembered earlier experiences, in the Brazilian Northeast, and I guessed what was going to

happen. I knew and expected that, suddenly, one of them, breaking the silence, would speak in his or her name and that of his or
her companions. I even knew the tenor of that discourse. And so
my own waiting, in the silence, must have been less painful than
it was for them to listen to the silence.

(*Hope*, 44–45)

Usually, Freire's interlocutors would say something to the
effect of: "You're the one who should have been talking, sir. You
know things, sir. We don't" (45) The "disconcerting silence" and
deference shown toward Freire are repetitions of authoritarian
relations these workers experienced in everyday life. The workers have transferred onto the person of Freire the position of
master. However, rather than avoid the transference, Freud and
psychoanalysis want to overcome the resistances "by making
mobile the energies which lie ready for the transference" (*SE*
12:143). There is no question that "controlling the phenomena
of transference presents . . . the greatest difficulties" (108), but
if handled properly, it affords the analyst a great advantage
since it is "expected to display to us everything in the way of
pathogenic instincts that is hidden in the patient's mind" (154).
Or, as Lacan puts it, "the transference is the enactment of the
reality of the unconscious" (*S* XI:146).

The more transference functions as resistance, the better
it enacts the reality of the unconscious—Freud writes: "Only
when the resistance is at its height can the analyst, working in
common with his patient, discover the repressed instinctual
impulses which are feeding the resistance; and it is this kind
of experience which convinces the patient of the existence and
power of such impulses" (*SE* 12:155). Thus, positive transference
will indeed result in conscious remembering, but relying solely
on positive transference "is a treatment by suggestion, and not a
psycho-analysis at all." "It only deserves the latter name," Freud
continues, "if the intensity of the transference has been utilized
for the overcoming of resistances" (143). When the transference
as resistance has been overcome or liquidated, the knowledge of
the unconscious, which has been turned from repetition into

conscious memory, remains: "Only then has being ill become impossible, even when the transference has once more been dissolved, which is its destined end." The implication for critical pedagogy is that so long as it adheres solely to the conscious form of remembering and closes itself off to the possibility of repetition, it depends upon positive transference, which makes it akin to suggestion—hence, its "repressive myths." By expanding the possibilities to include repetition, critical pedagogy is able to affect a more lasting form of learning, "For when it is all said and done, it is impossible to destroy anyone *in absentia* or *in effigie*" (108). On this account, the very flaw of critical pedagogy identified by Ellsworth—that it is imbued with the contradictions of the social conditions in which it is formed—turns out to be its very strength as it allows for the repetition of those contradictions thus allowing them to be overcome as a present-day force.

Psychoanalysis is not the only situation in which the transference is manifest. "As soon as the subject who is supposed to know exists somewhere," Lacan claims, "there is transference" (*S* XI:232). However, psychoanalysis is unique in that it draws its energies from the transference as resistance: "In each case we must wait until the disturbance of the transference by the successive emergence of transference-resistances has been removed" (*SE* 12:144). In analysis, transference itself is turned into the object under scrutiny by both the analyst and the analysand. This turning of transference into an observable object occurs through its function as resistance. Usually, it takes understanding how the analysand views the person of the analyst in order to turn transference from a relation into an object. Freud, in his case notes on the Ratman, gives an illustrative example of this process.[14] The Ratman, on Freud's diagnosis, harbors a death wish toward his father—an idea that the Ratman, of course, resists. Through the course of the analysis, the Ratman becomes increasingly anxious regarding Freud's interpretations until he "was obliged therefore to come by the conviction that his relationship to his father did indeed need to be amplified by material from the unconscious by the painful route of transference" (*Wolfman*, 164). As the transference takes shape, the Ratman relays "dreams, daytime fantasies and arbitrary notions," in which "he would insult" Freud while "at the same time he never intentionally showed [Freud] anything but the greatest respect." Freud takes notice that the Ratman's behavior becomes increasingly erratic. He would say to Freud, "Most honoured Professor, how can you allow yourself to be insulted in this way by filthy scum like me?" (164) while pacing about the room as if "he was putting himself at arm's length for fear that [Freud] would strike him" (165). Freud turns the Ratman's attention to his anxious behavior, and then the Ratman "recalled how his father would fall into sudden rages and in the violence of his feelings would no longer have any sense of how far he could go." The Ratman had transferred onto Freud's person the imago of his harsh father. The Ratman, in other words, was repeating his relationship with his father with Freud. Transference enables the Ratman to relive his unconscious relationship with his father in the present tense. Working through that transference-resistance, the Ratman "gradually gained the conviction he had been lacking."

If critical pedagogy wants students to become more aware of the problems of racism, sexism, classism, and other forms of oppression, then it must allow for the repetition of those relations within the controlled space of the classroom. As these forms of oppression are rooted in authoritarian relations, repeating them in the classroom will inevitably involve transferring authoritarian positions—the Patriarch, the Bourgeoisie, the Colonizer, the Bigot—onto the person of the teacher insofar as the teacher occupies the position of the "subject supposed to know." Acting as the recipient of the patient's various transferences is not a comfortable task, which is why Freud describes the transference as the most arduous of all the analyst's responsibilities. But it is the best way to learn the traumatic knowledge of the unconscious. In this way, taking on this transference can be seen an ethical decision, as Lacan says the "status of the unconscious . . . is ethical" (S XI:33). One must make an ethical decision to become the subject of the transference in order to achieve the ends of social justice. Critical pedagogy must follow Freud in saying: "Whatever it is, I must go there" (33).

6

Education by Way
of Truths: Lacan with Badiou

I

Jacques Lacan's diagram of the discourse of the analyst, as seen in Figure 6.1, presents a peculiarity in that it locates knowledge (S_2) in the position of truth. What does it mean to say that knowledge occupies the place of truth? In seminar XVII, Lacan himself recognizes that there is something deeply ambiguous in this idea: "We are properly speaking condemned to only being able, even on this point, still vague for us, about the relationship between knowledge and truth, to declare anything at all."[1] On the one hand, knowledge functions as truth in the sense that at the end of analysis the truth of the unconscious emerges. On the other hand however, Lacan senses something more at stake. In a lecture given a few years before seminar XVII entitled "Science and Truth," Lacan issues this challenge: "I will take it up now only to pose you analysts a question: does or doesn't what you do imply that the truth of neurotic suffering lies in having the truth as cause."[2] Here, Lacan suggests that what is important in psychoanalysis is that it deploys the function of "the truth as cause"—but the cause of what exactly? In seminar XVII, Lacan sheds some more light, claiming that the truth causes "only a collapse of knowledge" (*S* XVII:186). He goes on to say that it is a collapse that "creates a production" (186). More questions are begged: What is collapsed? What is produced? In the final meeting of seminar XVII, Lacan himself poses this question: "What sort of a disaster does analytic knowledge produce?" (191). Unfortunately, for us and for that year's seminarians, seminar XVII concludes without an answer.

$$\frac{a}{S_2} \xrightarrow{\text{A}} \frac{\$}{S_1}$$

Figure 6.1   The discourse of the analyst

So what we have is this: in the analytic discourse, knowledge and truth coincide. For Lacan, this means that in psychoanalysis the truth is cause: namely, the cause of a collapse in knowledge. But if it is a collapse, then it is a productive collapse as something new is learned from the unconscious. Analytic knowledge is thus a productive disaster.

To unpack the meaning of Lacan's claims, we turn to contemporary French philosopher Alain Badiou, for Badiou's thought most thoroughly works out how truth can function as the collapse and production of knowledge. Through a close reading of his *Ethics*,[3] Badiou's philosophy can serve as the key to understanding Lacan's cryptic statements about truth as cause. At the center of Badiou's thought is a radical reworking of the notion of truth and the implications of that reworking on knowledge. Badiou defines knowledge as "what transmits, what repeats."[4] In other words, knowledge is the collection of everything already known. Truth, on the other hand, is "something new"; more precisely, "the real process of a fidelity to," what he calls, "an event" (*Ethics*, 42). An event is, for Badiou, a contingent happening that intervenes within the realm of knowledge that forces a rethinking of that realm. Taken together, truth is what breaks through knowledge so that new knowledge can be created. Using Lacan's terms, truth causes the collapse of existing knowledge by revealing its limitations thus causing the possibility for the production of new knowledge. No doubt, Badiou's reassertion of truth will rub some the wrong way, especially in this age of cultural relativism. And Badiou, to a certain extent, intends his philosophy to be polemical. But much of the negative reaction to Badiou's use of truth can be forestalled by recognizing that he offers a reinvented notion of truth. For Badiou, truth is not substantive; rather, it is performative insofar as he defines it as "fidelity." Thus grasping the unique solution Badiou has to offer requires clarifying the distinction he makes between knowledge and truth.

Badiou makes another claim that is not irrelevant to the present discussion. In a short essay entitled "Art and Philosophy," Badiou writes, very briefly: "The meaning of 'education' is none other than . . . to organize knowledge to the extent that a certain truth can break through."[5] My claim is that Badiou's philosophy of truth embodies everything Lacan means with the claim that the truth is a cause. Furthermore, I claim that for both Badiou and Lacan, the primary location where truth and knowledge intersect is education.

II

In order to make intelligible the distinction Badiou makes between truth and knowledge, these two terms must be grasped within the wider context of his philosophical edifice. Since what is ultimately desired is the application of Badiou's truth/knowledge distinction to an educational context, we will not seek after a full commentary on his entire philosophical project but restrict ourselves to only those aspects that directly elucidate the relationship of truth and knowledge (so, for example, we will not touch the question of Badiou's use of mathematical set theory as a language of ontology).[6]

To begin with, life, Badiou argues, self-evidently presents itself as a situation of multiplicity:

> There are as many differences, say, between a Chinese peasant and a young Norwegian professional as between myself and anybody at all, including myself. . . . What we must recognize is that these differences hold no interest for thought, that they amount to nothing more than the infinite and self-evident multiplicity of humankind.
>
> (26)

That life is sheer multiplicity and difference can not only be observed anecdotally, but it has also been "proven" in such areas as mathematics, theoretical physics, and even art. All of these disciplines have shown in their own distinct way that its field comprises an infinite amount of possibilities. Badiou even suggests (following Deleuze and Guattari[7]) that, in fact, every individual person is in him- or herself already a multiple. Badiou calls "this kind of particular multiple," the "some-one" (*Ethics*, 44). And insofar as life is inhabited by a multitude of "some-ones," it is a "multiple of multiples" (25). Badiou calls this ensemble of the "multiple of multiples," the "situation": "Every situation, inasmuch as it is, is a multiple composed of an infinity of elements, each one of which is itself a multiple." Rather than a general description, one should think of the situation as a specific configuration of the "multiple of multiples." Thus there is no general situation as such but, rather, only particular situations in the plural.

Much like in Sartre's existentialism,[8] everything, for Badiou, happens within the specific context of a situation: "All humanity has its root in the identification in thought of singular situations" (*Ethics*, 16). Badiou cautions not to seek an ethics or truth in general: for him, there are no such things. Rather, one must only seek situational ethics and situational truths: "There are only—eventually—ethics of processes by which we treat the possibilities of a situation."

Thus Badiou's concern is not to play with the possibilities present in the multiplicity of the situation. To be sure, the number of ways the multiple can be arranged and rearranged is infinite, but it is also, in a certain sense, mundane. Rather than play with the situational possibilities, Badiou wants to radically reinvent the situation itself. To illustrate the specificity of Badiou's focus, imagine Leonardo da Vinci's *Mona Lisa*, framed and hanging on the wall in the Louvers. One way of transforming the *Mona Lisa* is by toying with the colors that comprise it. One can paint it all black. Or, one can paint it a rainbow assortment. Or, one can, a la Marcel Duchamp, paint a moustache on it. Each of these choices is indeed transgressive and alters the painting, but underneath these edits the *Mona Lisa* still remains, however defaced—or, if not the *Mona Lisa*, then, at least it remains a painting of some sort. Rather than play with the painting itself, Badiou wants to transform the *Mona Lisa* by altering the frame that houses it. He wants to take the frame apart and use its materials to create, say, a chair. With this one act, it is no longer the *Mona Lisa*; it cannot even be said to be a painting anymore—it is now a chair. It is in this spirit that Badiou understands his philosophical project.

Yet a situation, Badiou tells us, is not radically transformed of its own accord. If anything, a situation is allergic to change. Thus, for a situation to become radically changed, a supplement is required—"Let us call this *supplement* an *event* . . . which compels us to decide a new way of being" (41, original emphasis). What Badiou calls the "event" reveals that the current situation is not all and therefore is open to a complete overhaul. The event is therefore what "compels the subject to *invent* a new way of being and acting in the situation" (42, original emphasis). Because it compels a new way of being in the situation, the event breaks with the situation—or, put more precisely, it is the break itself. As a break, the event will appear from the standpoint of the situation as sheer nonsense—the event always "meant nothing according to the prevailing language and established knowledge of the situation" (43). However, since the situation establishes the parameters of Badiou's project, the event cannot be truly external to the situation. "It is thus an *imminent break*" (42, original emphasis). Thus the event has a peculiar relationship with the situation. On the one hand, the eventual break derives from some element within the situation. On the other hand, the situation does not recognize this element, as it differs from the established codes of knowledge. The event is, in other words, precisely impossible, but since the only possibility of radically transforming the situation lies in "*thinking* . . . the situation 'according to' the event" (41, original emphasis), one must affirm, at all costs, the "possibility of the impossible" (39).

III

Thus Badiou's entire philosophical project turns on the possibility of radically rewriting the situation by way of an event. Though an event opens up the possibility of rethinking the situation by revealing the point where its established knowledge no longer holds any consistency, it cannot do the transformative work by itself. The event can be repressed or suppressed in any number of ways. What is therefore necessary is for the event to take hold of an individual or individuals who will faithfully carry out the work of thinking the situation according to the event.

The process—for it is indeed a process—of maintaining fidelity to the event, of relating "henceforth to the situation *from the perspective of its evental supplement*" (41, original emphasis), is what Badiou calls a truth: "I shall call 'truth' (*a* truth) the real process of a fidelity to an event: that which this fidelity *produces* in the situation" (42, original emphasis). We must closely attend to three nuances of Badiou's concept of truth: truth is plural, nonsubstantial, and contingent.

First, note that Badiou does not insist on "the Truth," with a capital "T." With Badiou there is not one ultimate Truth. For Badiou, there are only truths in the plural—"*a* truth," as he is so quick to emphasize. Moreover, to the extent that a truth claims to be the total truth, it is, for Badiou, disaster, which is, in no uncertain terms, a form of evil: "Every absolutization of the power of a truth organizes an Evil" (85). The reason is that truths emerge within specific situations and concomitant to specific events. Now, within a given situation, it may happen that a singular event takes place, and under such circumstances, a single truth may be produced. But this does not exclude the possibility of multiple truths. For example, a single event may affect different individuals differently thus producing multiple truths in that sense. Or, a given situation may give rise to multiple events thus also producing multiple truths in that sense. And, finally, as one situation gives way to another, different, situation, the truths that are possible will change accordingly. To be sure, that Badiou insists upon the multiplicity of truths does not make truth relative, for, in every case, the truth is always a break with the existing situation. The key however is that none of these truths can lay claim to being the Truth nor should they be closed off to each other.

Second, truths, as one may have already noted, are not substantial. They are not, for example, statements that make a substantive claim, such as "God exists," "the United States is the Leader of the Free World," and so on. "A truth," Badiou writes, "is, first of all, something new" (61). Nothing substantive—that is to say, nothing with content—can be eternally new. Once something is turned into a substantive claim, it ceases to be new by definition. Badiou therefore gives the codification of newness a different name: knowledge. "What transmits," Badiou writes, "what repeats, we shall call *knowledge*" (61, original emphasis). For Badiou, a truth is a process. A process of what, exactly?—A process of radically reconfiguring, of rethinking, of reinventing our being in the situation that results from maintaining fidelity to an event and its implications. "Essentially," Badiou writes, "a truth is the material course traced, within the situation, by the eventual supplementation" (42). A truth is, in other words, the course of action individual subjects, guided by the event, take in a situation. Envisaged as a "material course," or as a process, Badiou uses the term "truth-process" interchangeably with "truth."

Against the idea that truths are timeless universals, Badiou advances the notion that they are contingent. Truths are not only contingent upon events taking place, but they are also contingent upon concrete individuals or "some-ones" taking up the cause of truth. Badiou calls the individual, "the bearer of a fidelity, the one who bears a process of truth" (43), the "subject," and, in this way, one can say that the "process of truth *induces* a subject" (43, original emphasis). And if the subject ever turns its back on a truth—infidelity or "betrayal" (78–80) being, for Badiou, a form of evil—truth itself collapses and is lost to nothingness. Hence, a truth-process requires an ethic of fidelity.

From here the uniqueness of Badiou's position on subjectivity is also visible. On the one hand, Badiou stands apart from the poststructuralists insofar as he maintains the reality of subjectivity. The subject, for Badiou, is not an "effect of structure." Rather, it is an actual phenomenological experience. On the other hand, Badiou stands apart from much of Western philosophy—from Descartes to Hegel—in that subjectivity is, for him, not transcendental. Rather, subjects are subjects of truths, that is, they emerge with truths, and truths are in turn contingent upon events and specific situations: "There is not, in fact, one single Subject, but as many subjects as there are truths" (28). Another unique feature of Badiou's theory of subjectivity is that the subject is not necessarily a single individual; it can be collective as well. Badiou's example here is love: "The lovers as such enter into the composition of *one* loving subject, who *exceeds* them both" (43, original emphasis). The event of falling in love causes two individuals to trace out a course of living in the situation as a single subject.[9] Thus the process of truth is not an endeavor of egotistical individualism but, rather, a collective experience. In fact, once a truth loses its universal openness, it ceases to be truth as such and turns instead into what is for Badiou a form of evil—namely, "Terror," or "simulacrum" (72–77).

To illustrate the subjectivizing truth-process, let us look at the four concrete areas or "subjective types" that Badiou identifies: science, art, love, and politics. We must mention that Badiou appears extremely restrictive in identifying only four areas where the truth-process takes place. Here, Badiou seems to be overly influenced by his teacher Louis Althusser, who has a similar quadripartite schema.[10] Badiou himself acknowledges the arbitrary nature of his four identified subjective types when he admits that the choices are personal: "As for me, I identify four fundamental subjective types" (28). But, more importantly, he leaves open the possibility that more "subjective types" exists than he admits, even going so far as to suggest that there are "as many subjective types as there are procedures of truth."

In all four subjective types, the situation is identified by a preexisting code of knowledge. Prior to Einstein, theoretical physics was dominated by a Newtonian paradigm. In art, prior to Schoenberg, only tonal music was thought to be possible. In love, prior to Romeo and Juliet, the situation was dominated by the Montague/Capulet family feud. And in France, prior to the student rebellions of May 1968, the political scene was a conservative situation. Then, in all four of these areas, an event takes place: Einstein discovers the general theory of relativity, Schoenberg composes experimental atonal pieces, Romeo and Juliet fall in love, and the students take to the streets. These events call forth or, using an Althusserian term, "interpellate" its respective subjects[11]: Einstein, Schoenberg's circle, Romeo and Juliet, and the collective student protesters. The implication of each of these events is nothing short of the revelation that the preexisting situation and its knowledge were inadequate: physics could not adequately grasp the dynamic nature of the universe, music was severely limited in its scope, a feud was not the only way these two families could relate, and the exclusion of workers' and students' rights was not a sufficient political situation. Having been seized by their respective events, the subjects need to rethink their situation in such a way that it becomes a completely new thing—they, in other words, must become subjects of truths. The results of the truth-processes are the creation of new situations and new knowledge: Einstein becomes the dominant paradigm in physics, Schoenberg's twelve-tone system becomes part of the musical canon, Romeo and Juliet's love mends the warring families, and the French political apparatus is forced to recognize workers' and students' rights.

IV

When Badiou writes "distinguishing truth from knowledge is essential" (61), he is certainly right. However, these two must not be distinguished at the expense of diminishing the value of either. That is to say, it is altogether too reductive to say that truth is good while knowledge is bad. For example, in what sense would Newtonian physics or tonal music be "bad"? Rather, the terms "truth" and "knowledge" must be grasped dialectically, that is to say, as dependent upon one another's existence. Thus Badiou's claim that truth is the "sole known source of new knowledges" (70) must be counterbalanced with the reminder that truth cannot exist without preexisting knowledge. Truths are not created ex nihilo— as Badiou himself reminds us: "There is no heaven of truths" (43). As such, the value of knowledge cannot be understated.

One must tread carefully, especially since Badiou's language often seems to emphasize truth at the exclusion of knowledge. Knowledge, as Badiou describes it, is characteristically homeostatic. Therefore a "truth-process is heterogeneous to the instituted knowledges of a situation" (43). The main danger in knowledge is when its practitioners raise it to a transcendent level thus refusing to entertain that truths can come into existence. The only problem is if a teacher puts a doctrine of knowledge onto a pedestal and disciplines students into accepting it as the only way. And though this tendency toward homeostasis might manifest in the adherents of existing knowledge preventing or repressing any and all evental discovery (for example, the church's stance towards Galileo), enmity need not always be the case. For example, the state was not actively trying to suppress Einstein's discoveries. Homeostasis is sometimes achieved by preexisting knowledge's ignorance as to the reality of its own contingency—knowledge is often simply unaware that truths are possible. Moreover, a truly great discovery cannot even be registered unless it is placed against the background of some preexisting knowledge. Thus what is so special in Schoenberg is only intelligible if juxtaposed with what is so canonical in Mozart. The possibility therefore exists that adherents of knowledge can respond favorably to a truth or even work cooperatively to bring one about.

And as preexisting knowledge is the necessary precondition for truths, truths themselves complete the circle by resulting in new knowledge. The circle is squared and the dialectic is complete as truths are eventually codified into knowledge and the previous situation is lifted onto a higher plane thus constituting a new situation. Then, the process presumably starts all over again with new events disrupting the findings of previous truth-processes (for example, quantum physicists, like Neils Bohr, go beyond Einstein's discoveries). Grasping truths and knowledge as dialectical movement will be important for developing a pedagogy based on Badiouian principles.

V

What Badiou means when he claims "education is feasible only by way of truths"[12] should now be discernable. Education is not about the event itself. Notice that Badiou uses the term "truth," not "event." Keep in mind that an event is the contingent occurrence that announces the inadequacy of the realm of knowledge. The event allows for a truth-process to emerge and for subjects to grab hold of that process. If Badiou had written that the meaning of education was to enable an event to take place, then pedagogy's role would be to show the limitations of the curriculum, to criticize the established ways of conducting education, and to alert students to the way knowledge represses creativity and newness. In short, pedagogy of the event would be a subtractive gesture, an act of decompletion, or a process of tearing away from the codified presentation of knowledge so that an event can take place in the classroom.[13]

In using the term "truth," Badiou suggests something different than the subtractive forms of pedagogy described above. Here, pedagogy is not so interested in attuning students to the inadequacy of the regimes of knowledge. Rather, pedagogy aims to facilitate the students' fidelity to an event that has already taken place. As truth is the process of radically transforming the situation according to the event, pedagogy facilitates evental fidelity by helping students think through the existing situation of knowledge according to that event. Pedagogy allows knowledge to be (re)thought through the lens of the event thus allowing the creation of new knowledge. Pedagogy is here envisioned in a supportive role.

The main burden of learning—that is, the transformation of the situation by the faithful rethinking of knowledge according to the event thus resulting in the creation of new knowledge—falls on the student. The student is the one who must be seized by an event of their own accord. The teacher's role is not to enforce an event. Nor is the teacher even to initiate a truth-process, much less give direction to its course. Everything as far as an event and what a truth is belongs to the student. The teacher's responsibility is to present knowledge, and to present it in such a way that students can incorporate it within their truth-process, that is, to rethink it. While the "pedagogy of truth" might appear diminished in form, it plays perhaps the most crucial role, for the students' truth-process, like any burgeoning newness, is in all likelihood fragile, and it can be squashed if the teacher or anyone else were insistent upon their authority as bearers of knowledge. This is where standardization and standardized testing are extremely detrimental mechanisms to student-learning: the authoritative and unchallengeable appearance of standardized knowledge serves to reinforce the immutability of knowledge, which militates against the truth-process.[14] In contrast, the teacher should use all of their pedagogical skill to present knowledge in such a way that students feel comfortable challenging it and rethinking it according to the event that has taken hold of them. An example may be helpful. Think of a student who has encountered an event that reveals to them that the existing canon of literature unjustly excludes the artistic production of many authors from different ethnic, racial, gender, and sexual backgrounds. The teacher's role, in this case, is not to suggest this idea to the student: to do so has the danger of incurring a form of Evil. But neither is it the teacher's role to discourage a student who has been seized by this event. Rather, the teacher is to teach the existing canon, along with supplemental materials—through dialogue, lecture, discussion, projects, and whatever other techniques one has at their disposal—in such a way that the student can think through the implications this event has for the preexisting forms of knowledge. Hopefully, the truth-process is ongoing, with one teacher providing a bridge to the next. For students who have not been seized by an event, the teacher's presentation may help them to see that knowledge is never all and that something new is still possible. The final outcome of this pedagogy of truth, in either case, will be the production of new knowledge that transforms the preexisting canon.

It is now plainly visible why truth and knowledge must be seen dialectically. Fidelity to an event is the sole domain of the student. Meanwhile, pedagogy contributes knowledge to that process of fidelity as so much grist for the truth-mill. Because truth and knowledge are dialectically related, one participant is not more or less important to the educational process than the other. Both are equally necessary.

Because the teacher and the student both contribute to the pedagogical process in different but essential ways, it is necessary to conceive of them as a single subject. Recall that for Badiou the subject of truth is not necessarily a single individual—it appears that the teacher-student relationship qualifies as one of those cases. The collective potential of Badiou's subject becomes important in the classroom. Much like in Badiou's example of love where two become a singular subject, the pedagogical relationship also conjoins the teacher and the student into a singular subjectivity.[15] However, subjective relations abound in the classroom. Keep in mind that, for Badiou, there are as many subjective types as there are truths. Thus multiple and nonconforming truth-processes might take place within a single classroom. In this case, the pedagogy of truth should not seek to collapse the disjunctive truth-processes—that is to say, truth-processes should not be standardized—but, rather, their uniqueness should be honored and preserved. In so doing, the teacher enters into a subjective relationship with each distinctive truth-process while at the same time *not* serving as a way in which the different student-subjects of truths are collapsed. The teacher can be connected to every truth-process while the truth-processes themselves remain distinct. On the other side, a true truth-process is, for Badiou, universally open,[16] and therefore, other students may join in a particular ongoing truth-process, or distinct truth-processes can converge to form alliances on their own accord. If any of these scenarios were to occur, the students involved would become subjects together. The teacher serves as a conduit for such interactions to take place.

VI

Pedagogy can play another supportive function: guide students away from Evil. For Badiou, the truth-process is beset on all sides by opposing forces. Keeping in mind that knowledge is not inherently bad, these opposing forces should not be conceived as enemies but more as friction. But as friction, these opposing forces have the effect of slowing, even dissipating, the truth-process. However, Badiou identifies three distinct ways the truth-process can collapse so that the end result is more than friction. Indeed, these three ways are, for him, Evil.

It is important to keep in mind that in the same manner truth is not general but situation specific, Evil too is not general but only meaningful in the context of a truth-process, as its very transgression. The three forms of Evil, which have been referenced throughout the present essay, are simulacrum or terror, betrayal, and disaster.

"Not every 'novelty,'" Badiou warns, "is an event" (*Ethics*, 72). Badiou's example is the Nazis. The Nazis were indeed a novelty, but they were not in any way, shape, or form an event or subjects of a truth-process. What then is the difference? As an event is a contingent occurrence that announces the lack of the situation, what Badiou describes as "a kind of flashing supplement that happens to the situation" (72), it follows that "what is retained of it in the situation, and what serves to guide the fidelity, must be something like a trace, or a name, that refers back to the vanished event" (72). Anything that tries to preserve the event through its symbolization turns the event into a simulacrum. The result of a simulacrum is terror. The Nazis are Evil in the strong sense because they legitimized themselves by making reference to the Bolshevik Revolution—hence, National *Socialism*—through its symbolization in the swastika. That is to say, the Nazis presented themselves as the codification of the genuine socialist revolution of the working person's party and in so doing become the living embodiment of Evil.

Why can an event not be symbolized? Why must it remain in the form of the trace? The reason, Badiou suggests, "is precisely the fact that it relates to the particularity of a situation only from the bias of its void" (73). What the event announces is the lack in the existing situation of knowledge. In other words, the event points out a void. As the reference to a void, it itself cannot be substantial. Any attempt to add substance to an event can only be a simulacrum or a semblance—a cover that falsely embodies a void. The danger in the simulacrum is more than the presentation of a lie. It has material consequences. Once substance is attributed to the event, the imposter-event prescribes who can be its subjects—namely, those who embody the same substance. In the example of the Nazis, their Evil gesture of placing an image to the event—namely, the German people—precluded Jews, socialists, gypsies, homosexuals, and others from becoming subjects of truth. The Nazi simulacrum becomes the Nazi terror. Though all attempts to symbolize the event will not fall into the extermination of millions of people, they remain in their integral structure, Evil.

A simulacrum can indeed take place in the classroom. Any time a student substantiates their project by symbolizing an event, they fall into Evil. Hubris and exclusivity usually accompany the simulacrum. Students who follow a simulacrum oftentimes see themselves as somehow better than other students or the teacher. They also feel that only they have a right to understand what they are engaged in. The reason they see this difference is that they believe they have some privileged access to an event that took place in another place or in another time ("I read this book once, and so now I know more than you"; "I took a class with this famous person, and so I am more legitimate than you"; "I hold a special degree, and so I am more privileged than you"; and so on). Often times, the symbol that substantiates the event for them is easy to see (the book, the teacher, the degree, etc.). Only those who share this substance (have read that book, learned with that teacher, hold that degree, etc.) have a part with their simulacrum. Pedagogy must work against the hubris of the simulacrum. Pedagogy must strive to dismantle its claims to privilege. It must separate the truth-events from simulacra. It can do this by uncovering its signs of pride and exclusion. The truth-event is never symbolizeable, and therefore it is humble and universally open to all. The simulacrum is arrogant and thrives by drawing lines between who do and do not share its substance.

The second form of Evil is betrayal. Because all truth-processes face an inherent amount of friction, it is tempting to abandon the difficult process of rewriting the situation according to its perspective. It can be abandoned or betrayed. The act of betrayal is, for Badiou, Evil. Pedagogy must edify the student. It must encourage them to remain faithful to the event that seized them. It must say to them: "'Keep going!' Keep going even when you have lost the thread, when you no longer feel 'caught up' in the process, when the event itself has become obscure" (79). It seems that in a time of high standardization, pedagogy must encourage students to remain faithful to the truth-process and not betray the event more than ever before.

The third form of Evil is disaster. Truths, keep in mind, are always situation specific. There is, for Badiou, no truth in general. To believe that a truth-process has "the ability to name and evaluate *all* the elements of the objective situation" turns it into a disaster. Disaster is a genuine truth-process run amok. "Rigid and dogmatic," the disastrous truth-event "would claim the power, based on its own axioms, to name the whole of the real, and thus to change the world" (83). A student might believe that they have the answer to everything and that their answer is better and more qualified than others. In fact, this student might believe they know it all by virtue of the truth-process. Such a student has turned their truth-process into a disaster. Pedagogy should act to temper the student, to impart with the student the sense of modesty as to how far the truth-process actually extends.

For Badiou, truth invents a new way of being in the situation, truth produces new knowledge. This truth is able to exist because the previous regime of knowledge was shown to be incomplete. So it is with Lacan's discourse of the analyst. The discourse of the analyst describes the social links that must be configured in order for truth to play this dual causal function as subtraction from the previous regime of knowledge and production of new knowledge. What configures the situation into the discourse of the analyst is the event, a contingent traversal of the imaginary functions that drown out the unconscious. Pedagogy represents the excessive object that the previous regimes of knowledge cannot take into account, an object that opens up and sustains the truth as cause.

7

Lessons of Love: On Pedagogical Love

I

From the beginning, philosophers as different as Plato and Paulo Freire have claimed that love plays an integral part in education and pedagogy. This role has been formulated in many ways: love has the power to inspire students to seek after knowledge, love can unite the teacher and student in the quest for knowledge, and the love of learning can even empower students to challenge knowledge thereby pushing its limits. Though love has long been posited to be a positive force in the processes of teaching and learning, two recent phenomena have called the necessity of love into question: namely, teacher-student sexual scandal and the standardization movement. Each phenomenon highlights a different problematic that is associated with love: sexual scandal points to the vague line between love and sex, while the standardization of knowledge and increased reliance on standardized testing implicitly devalue love as being irrelevant and even damaging for its potential to bias the assessment of student work.

Let us begin with teacher-student sex.[1] To be sure, teacher-student sexual scandal is not a recent development, but the recent proliferation of reports of such scandals in the news media and popular culture is alarming. Of particular concern is not the quantity of stories but their increasingly perverse and disturbing quality. Take, for example, the 1999 scandal of Florine Maria Strimel, a special-education teacher who had a sexual relationship with a runaway seventeen-year-old student, for which she was subsequently imprisoned. Strimel not only had a sexual relationship with the seventeen-year-old special-education student, but she was also able to obtain $3,000 that the student took from his parents, thereby adding insult to injury.[2] Where others may see this as a clear case of sexual impropriety, Strimel and the student both claimed, at some point, to genuinely be in love. What makes this case typical of most love relationships between teacher and student is how so-called true love always seems to fall back into the sexual realm. Strimel's case is also a lesson about how love, as commonly understood, maintains a tenuous boundary with sex so that its inclusion within the pedagogical relationship—one supposed to be free of sexuality—remains problematic. The arresting police officer Rick Young best summarizes the problematic of love and pedagogy with this understatement: "This is a misuse of authority by a teacher taking advantage of a young man's emotions."[3] The point here is not to further condemn Strimel, nor is it to attempt an explanation for the causes of her behavior; this story highlights not the extreme danger that lies within the question of love but the danger that lies in wait when this question goes unresolved and unanswered.

While Strimel's case is an object lesson of the porous boundary between love and sex, the film *Election* exemplifies another important lesson: the ambiguities between love and what is often considered love's opposite, hate.[4] *Election* is the story of civics teacher, Jim McAllister, who both loves his students and is loved by them—until he is confronted with Tracy Flick, an overly ambitious student whose affair with McAllister's colleague results in the colleague's dismissal. Out of fear of ending up like his colleague, McAllister develops feelings that seem to be the opposite position of love, nursing a deep hatred for Flick (which, in a twist, results in his dismissal). What we learn about love and hate from *Election* is one of the fundamental lessons of psychoanalysis: namely, that hatred is not the opposite of love and sexual desire but its other side, since love is fundamentally ambivalent. Though McAllister changes the way his desire for

Flick is expressed, his hatred does not challenge or transform the underlying fact of their relation—that his feelings are motivated by sexual desire. (This connection also raises the question of whether or not the love McAllister shows his other students truly is devoid of sexuality.) In other words, while McAllister initially appears to be Strimel's opposite (in being motivated by hatred instead of love), from the psychoanalytic point of view—which holds that love and hate are simply two sides of the same coin—McAllister actually stands *with* Strimel. Underneath their differences, McAllister and Strimel are alike in that sexual desire structures their pedagogical relationships.

Though cases such as Strimel's and her fictional counterpart McAllister's problematize love, it is the state's emphasis on standardization that demonstrates how more is at stake in the question of love than just simply love itself. For the state, learning standards represent the complete set of knowledge with which education should be concerned. Accordingly, teachers need only teach to the standards as impartially as possible. If love is to exist in education at all, it can only play a peripheral role—that of motivating students to perform to the best of their abilities in the acquisition of knowledge and to display this knowledge on standardized tests. But if love is merely a factor in motivating students to acquire knowledge, then it is not only problematic but also potentially damaging: as a form of motivation, love is capable of transforming only the manner in which knowledge is taught and learned, not the *content* of what is being learned. For example, take the cliché of the teacher who "makes learning fun"—all of the particular expressions of the funny teacher's love (jokes, anecdotes, illustrations, and the like) do not challenge the content of the lessons. Perhaps now more than ever, in an era of standardization, we should insist upon a form of love that does not promote the reproduction of knowledge but, instead, is capable of transforming it. But the lesson learned from the sexual scandals is that establishing the legitimacy of love in the teaching relation requires that we differentiate it from sexuality.[5]

II

There are many positions surrounding the question of pedagogical love, but here I will focus on three:

1. The erotic position. Love not only plays an important role in teaching knowledge, it plays the essential role. One should not be afraid of love's slippage into the domain of sexuality, because it is precisely through this slippage that love realizes its full pedagogical potential.
2. The caring position. Just as in the erotic position, love plays an essential role for teaching knowledge, but, unlike the erotic position, love can play this role only insofar as it is not sexual. What allows love to accomplish this is its affective dimension, not sexual desire.
3. The technical position. Education is really about hard-and-fast knowledge, and, as such, love is inappropriate to education since it might lead to bias. Love is dangerous.

In contrast with these three standard views, I will advance a fourth: love as conceived by psychoanalysis—in particular, the schema of love given by Jacques Lacan.

As we saw in our discussion of *Election*, by clarifying that love is fundamentally ambivalent, psychoanalysis is able to shed light on the question of love and its discontents. In his seminar *Encore*, Lacan gives his shocking, even absurd, thesis on love: love comes as a supplement for the nonexistence of a sexual relationship.[6] What could he possibly mean by this? Let us begin by briefly introducing Lacan's theory of sexual difference in relation to his bold and contentious statement "There is no such thing as a sexual relationship." Here he is not suggesting that sexual intercourse as a biological reality does not exist, but rather that the symbolic positions of the two sexes are always separated by an insurmountable disjunction. The social order is made up of two symbolic positions whose reconciliation, either by unifying them into one sexual position or by finding a third mediating position, is nonexistent. This is to say that the two sexes are

irreconcilable in that any attempt at finding the perfect media-
tion between these two symbolic positions results in failure. In
this precise way, it is possible to conceptualize sexual intercourse,
though it is a biological reality, as something that is not "real" but
imaginary insofar as sex can be used to cover the trauma of the
symbolic disjunction of the two sexes. Keeping in mind that
Lacan gave this statement during the historical moment of the
Sexual Revolution of the 1960s and 1970s, it should be read as a
criticism of the notion that sexual experimentation could close
the distance of sexual difference as well as put an end to social
antagonisms. In fact, we can read the declaration "There is no
such thing as a sexual relationship" as a critique of the notion
that *any* relationship, sexual or otherwise, can be reconciled by
conforming the relation with an ideal third position, for that
ideal is ultimately an imagined ideal.

For Lacan, therefore, the social world is constituted by the
antagonism of sexual difference, and there is no "third term"
that might represent a healed and closed sociosymbolic space.
And if the union of the two sexes is barred—or as he puts it,
if there is no such thing as a sexual relationship—then love, in
his view, is a sign of this failure: "What makes up for the sexual
relationship is, quite precisely, love" (*S* XX:45).

The Lacanian thesis that love arises as a supplement for the
lack of a sexual relationship can be read in two ways. The first
way is to understand love as something that supplements the
failure of the sexual relationship by covering or, making up
for, this failure. For instance, Lacan observes, "As a specular
mirage, love is essentially deception" (*S* XI:268), and "Love is
impotent, though mutual, because it is not aware that it is but
the desire to be One, which leads us to the impossibility of
establishing the relationship between 'them-two'" (6). Here,
two people attempt to achieve an ideal oneness by way of love,
a oneness that ultimately proves to be a deception, a chimerical
lure. Or, put another way, love is an attempt to make a sexual
relationship where there is none. Rather than taking the impossibility of an ideal relationship into account as the status of their
relationship as such, love becomes a relationship in the imaginary

register—that is, love becomes the method through which the subject identifies with the other insofar as they are similar (the narcissism of love) or different (the ambivalence of love).

The second way to read Lacan's thesis is that love should not be seen as an imaginary screen that covers the disjunction of the sexes but, rather, as something that announces this disjunction—that is, a supplementality whose existence draws attention to the disjunction as such. Toward the end of *Encore*, Lacan himself begins to theorize the possibility of such a love: "For it is love that approaches being as such in the encounter. Isn't it in love's approach to being that something emerges that makes being into what is only sustained by the fact of missing each other?" (*S* XX:145). Here, love represents a restructuring of the relationship of the sexes precisely by taking their disjunction as constitutive of their relationship—what Lacan refers to as "them-two." Disjunction is what enables the two to be "them-two," without resorting to identification, which as an imaginary relation is always subject to dissolution. This second account of love provides the basis for theorizing a teacher-student love that neither falls into sexuality nor is a cover for reproducing dominant knowledge.

In his essay "What is Love?" Alain Badiou effectively draws out the meaning of the second account of Lacanian love when he asserts, "Love is an enquiry of the world from the point of view of the Two, and not an enquiry of each term of the Two about the other."[7] As a relationship of two—as opposed to a relationship of imaginary oneness—both partners in love seek knowledge not from the other (which would be identification) but from the world. We must be careful not to interpret Badiou as suggesting an absolute disjunction—as if, "them-two" have no part in each other. Rather, for Badiou, love is the event that structures the "them-two," or, as he put it in his unpublished seminar "On Love," love gives the "them-two" a new sense of the Two.[8] In this way, love also describes the lovers' process of inquiring into the world from their distinctive positions, a process that enables them to view the world from the new standpoint of collective subjectivity. Love structures the truth of the sexual relationship—that it is a relationship constituted by a disjunction—and this truth enables the parties to undertake such an inquiry. Rather than providing the path for one party to pass knowledge to the other—which would be a denial of the fundamental disjunction—love becomes a path for both to seek knowledge from the world together. Clearly, this leads to a different view of the teacher-student relation.

III

At first glance, the erotic position is very provocative, and for this reason easy to dismiss, yet it is this very provocation that raises the crucial question: what is at stake when eros is not allowed in the classroom?[9] Perhaps bell hooks provides the best response: "To restore passion to the classroom or to excite it in classrooms where it has never been, professors must find again the place of eros within ourselves and together allow the mind and body to feel and know desire."[10] Central to this notion of pedagogy is its intent to incite the student's desire to learn and pursue knowledge, not for knowledge's sake, but because that knowledge will be transformative for the student in terms of how the student thinks about the world. Such an understanding of transformative learning creates the potential for altering the structures of oppression that are reproduced by dominant frames of knowledge: incited by eros, students unabashedly question the self-apparent nature of official knowledge.[11] Furthermore, by allowing eros to enter the classroom, the classroom space is itself transformed into a space where crucial knowledge—and, for hooks, the transformation of oppression—can be pursued.

In hooks's view, an eroticized pedagogy does not mean a sexualized pedagogy but one that is passionate and inspiring. Still, hooks recognizes the potential for an eroticized pedagogy to slip into sexuality, but she warns against fearing such a slippage. In fact, she theorizes the intersection of love and sex to be a site of empowerment:

> To understand the place of eros and eroticism in the classroom, we must move beyond thinking of those forces solely in terms of the sexual, though that dimension need not be denied.[12]

While it is important that we name and vigilantly challenge abuses of power wherein the erotic becomes the terrain of exploitation and/or oppression, it is equally important for us to acknowledge the erotic as a site of empowerment and positive transformation. Eroticism, even that which leads to romantic involvement between professors and students, is not inherently destructive.[13]

Jane Gallop develops this idea further in her provocative book *Feminist Accused of Sexual Harassment,* which argues that sexualizing pedagogy is a crucial component for learning.[14] Like hooks, Gallop maintains that love intensifies the desire to learn, but she goes beyond hooks in asserting that the crucial turn is when love becomes sexualized. Sexuality breaks down the power differential between a teacher and a student, and the teacher becomes for the student not a possessor of infallible knowledge but a mortal whose knowledge has limits. Combined with this vision of the professor or teacher as just a person, the student's passion to learn is not quelled, but indeed given greater vigor and courage. The courage that derives from sexual pedagogy takes on special significance when the knowledge the teacher embodies is the dominant ideology. According to this account, students inspired by love are no longer inclined simply to accept the teacher's presentation of knowledge; they will have the confidence to challenge it. Here, one sees how Gallop's self-proclaimed "spectacle" raises a very serious point: namely, that the dimension of sexuality cannot be denied. In her analysis, however, she seems to overlook the other powerful dimension of love: while love can make a person in power vulnerable and appear mortal, it also can cause one to idealize the other, covering over the loved object's imperfections. One must always keep in mind Sigmund Freud's caution: "In connection with this question of being in love we have always been struck by the phenomenon of sexual overvaluation—the fact that the loved object enjoys a certain amount of freedom from criticism."[15] It is important to note that both Gallop and hooks are discussing the performance of an erotic pedagogy in the university setting. This begs the question of whether an erotic pedagogy can work in K-12 education. The dangers here are obvious. But if an erotic pedagogy promotes passion and excitement for learning, then should we not at the very least consider the possibility of the erotic (if not the sexual) in K-12 teaching? The Strimel case exemplifies the danger of exploitation and the abuse of authority. This danger only increases when one considers the possibility of an erotic pedagogy with younger students. Consider the case of Mary Kay Letourneau, who some years ago had an affair with a fourteen-year-old student, for instance.[16] In cases like those of Strimel and Letourneau, the eroticization of the teacher-student relation did not have the kind of transformative effect Gallop and hooks envisioned. It may appear, therefore, that a pedagogy of love in the K-12 context should keep the line between sexuality and love distinct. But trying to recommend an erotic pedagogy that keeps a safe distance from sexuality denies the fact that the connection with sexuality is what makes an erotic pedagogy effective.

Of course, there is also the simple reality that the law restricts sexuality by prohibiting sex with minors. But does transgressing this law result in its subversion? In *Civilization and its Discontents*, for instance, Freud showed that for society to preserve itself from the problem of human aggression, it must inhibit the libido by restricting human sexuality, which leads to its satisfaction through the formation of libidinal ties with others in the community in the form of friendship.[17] The aggression left unfulfilled by the imposition of the law's prohibition is taken up by the ego and turned against itself; this is the superego. Thus the paradox of obeying the law is that the more we obey the law, the more aggression is taken up by the superego and turned back upon the ego, and then the guiltier we feel—such is the inherent discontent of civilization. To illustrate this logic, let us return to *Election*. McAllister's guilt is produced precisely by his obedience to the prohibition on sex with Flick. Rather than resulting in tranquility and satisfaction, McAllister's obedience increases his discontent, which ultimately results in his desire resurfacing in the form of aggression and hatred.

Upon closer inspection, we see that, for psychoanalysis, transgression does not result in the subversion of the law, nor is the superego-guilt that comes with the law bypassed. On this point, Lacan is clear: "Transgression in the direction of *jouissance* only takes place if it is supported by the oppositional principle, by the forms of the Law" (*S* VII:177, original emphasis). Since transgression is ultimately sustained by the oppositional force of the law, there exists an enjoyment in transgression itself, and this surplus enjoyment is what Lacan calls jouissance. The jouissance of transgression results from knowing that our transgression will never eradicate the law. If it did, we would be eliminating the conditions for our own transgression and, hence, the source of our jouissance. Transgression can only produce jouissance as long as something exists to be violated. So, rather than being a barrier against jouissance, the law supports it by inciting transgression. That is to say, law and transgression are in a dialectical relation rather than in an oppositional one, and this dialectic prevents an erotic pedagogy from being transformative for K-12 education.

The erotic position's value lies in its theorization of sexuality as a site of empowerment insofar as it possesses the power to neutralize the teacher's symbolic position. We could summarize this potential for empowerment as follows: erotic pedagogy displaces the teacher from his or her symbolic location, thereby closing the power gap that separates the teacher from the student; that is, erotic pedagogy closes the distance separating the symbolic locations of teacher and student by creating an imaginary relationship—in this case, the sexual relationship. The promise held out by sexuality is the old promise of creating a unity from two positions, a oneness.

In discussing sexuality, Lacan distinguishes between the object of desire and the object that causes desire, which he calls *objet petit a* or object *a*. This distinction explains how desire is sustained even after it has attained its object. For example, in sexuality, though desire achieves its object (sex with the other), desire is not eradicated; rather, it is sustained because the object of desire is not the object that causes desire. The understanding of love as an imaginary relationship with the other conflates these two objects—that is, we identify with the other insofar as we identify the other with the cause of our desire. Using Lacan's schema of the object of desire and the *objet petit a*, we might say that the traditional teacher-student relationship, where the teacher's power is unchallenged and the student acquires the knowledge issued by the teacher, looks something like this: the object of desire is the teacher's knowledge, while the object that causes the student's desire is something more elusive, such as success in school, validation, and so on. In contrast, the erotic position formulates the teacher-student relation more like this: the teacher as a sexual object is the object of the student's desire, while the object that causes the student's desire is something more elusive—perhaps it is oneness, the closure of the power gap, or knowledge. Indeed, erotic pedagogy results in something different in the student's desire—specifically, the student no longer desires official knowledge—but this is not because sexuality represents a radical restructuring of the teacher-student relation. Rather, erotic pedagogy shifts the object of desire from official knowledge to something else (teacher's personal opinion, transformation of power structures, stances against race/gender/ sexual oppression) while leaving the very coordinates of the teacher-student relationship in tact. This raises the question: what if a teacher with a differing political/ethical stance than that of Gallop or hooks teaches with the same erotic passion? Or, put more crudely, what if a teacher uses erotic love for evil rather than good? What seems to be in order, then, and what theorists of eros cannot address, is a love that does not simply substitute objects of desire but that radically restructures the teacher-student relationship.

Again, at stake is not just sexuality but knowledge. While sexuality can alter the power differential between teacher and student, this can still be the basis for teaching knowledge that does not result in the kind of transformation hooks and Gallop favor. Take the examples of Strimel and Letourneau: in both cases, the teacher and student believed themselves to have found a new relationship by using sex to break through the network of power that constituted their old relationship; however, in these cases, sexuality did not bring about the kind of structural change in the teacher-student relation that would result in student's questioning official knowledge. On the contrary, sexuality could not provide a space for challenging the teacher's power and knowledge. It provided one for accepting it.

IV

If the erotic position fully engages love without flinching at the ambiguous relation between love and sex—even, at times, embracing this ambiguity—then the discourse of care gives an account of love that attempts to draw a line between love as affect and love as sex.[18] Advocates of caring pedagogy criticize the notion that pedagogy does not have or need an affective dimension; at the same time, however, they recognize the potential for love to turn into sexual desire. Caring pedagogy is positioned as a middle ground in between these two poles—a "third way." Angela Valenzuela describes care in the following way: "The composite imagery of caring that unfolds accords moral authority to teachers and institutional structures that value and actively promote respect and a search for *connection*, between teacher and student and among students themselves."[19] By describing care to be a relationship of connection and respect, how does Valenzuela guarantee that care might not become sexual desire? This is to ask, is the cut that divides love into two parts—care and sexual desire—ever clean enough? Lacan would certainly complicate such a clean cut, as well as the binary partitions that result from it, by claiming that these partitions are imagined rather than structural. My contention is neither with the attempt to formulate a loving pedagogy nor with the intentions that drive this attempt, but with the specific method used to accomplish this task—that is, the reliance upon a clean cut between care and sexual desire.

Before we turn to the question of this distinction, we should understand another crucial component to caring pedagogy. According to Valenzuela, two kinds of care exist: aesthetic care and authentic care. Aesthetic care is concerned with, what she calls, the technical aspects of education (knowledge, grades, behavior, and so on): "Schools are structured around an *aesthetic* caring whose essences lies in attention to things and ideas" (*Subtractive*, 23, original emphasis). Against aesthetic care, Valenzuela gives a second account of care—*authentic* care, which "emphasizes relations of reciprocity between teachers and students" (61). The proper pedagogy of care is the one that passes from aesthetic to authentic care, a transition marked by the establishment of reciprocity: "When the *cared-for* individual responds by demonstrating a willingness to reveal her/his essential self, the reciprocal relation is complete" (21, original emphasis).

In considering this view of care, we must remember Freud's observation that every social relation is libidinally invested; thus, a minimal sexual reality exists in every relation, even in the most platonic: "It is well known how easily erotic wishes develop out of emotional relations of a friendly character, based upon appreciation and admiration."[20] Paradoxically, the very insistence that care strive for a purely asexual relation affirms Freud's point that it is libidinally invested. Freud warned that part of the connection between a teacher and student, part of its very relation of reciprocity, is invested with sexual desire. While the issue of sex is nowhere to be seen on the surface of care—that is, care is always described as a relation of platonic "respect" or general "affect"—it is possible that this repressed kernel of sexuality will return in the form of the "essential self."

To illustrate this point, take the film *Rushmore*, which tells the story of a teacher, Rosemary Cross, who befriends a student, Max Fischer.[21] By all accounts, Fischer and Cross's friendship qualifies as an authentically caring relation, and, in fact, it is this caring relation that inspires Fischer to achieve minimal academic success. Fischer must repress the sexual desire he feels for Cross for the sake of their friendship. At the crucial moment when Fischer initiates the passage of their friendship to a deeper level of care, he reveals his essential self to Cross, but, in a twist, what emerges as Fischer's essential self is his repressed sexual desire for her. While some might presume that sexual desire, once placed under the control of the conscious will, eventually dissipates, the lesson we learn from *Rushmore* is that this never occurs. Instead, sexual desire lies in wait in the unconscious.

For Valenzuela, the essential self can be many things, and this point highlights how care might make education something more than merely the reproduction of dominant knowledge. Students are often frustrated with how the institution of education systematically fails them, according to Valenzuela a failure that demonstrates the persistence of racist power structure both in school and in society at large. Rather than voice their frustration, many students bury and hide these feelings. This frustration with the institutional forms of discrimination and oppression (which Valenzuela's study identifies as racism, but which can include gender, sexual, or class inequalities as well) become the students' essential self. When the teacher can tap into this deeply guarded kernel of frustration, and when the student trusts the teacher enough to reveal this essential self, their relation passes from an aesthetically caring one to an authentically caring one. It is important to note that this essential self, while it can take many forms, very often is characterized by frustration, apathy, hatred, or some other disturbed emotion. It is equally important to recognize that there is one form the essential self cannot take: sexual desire. If it takes this form, revealing the self would not result in authentic caring but would lead to the disintegration of the caring relation as such. This is what we see in the disclosure Fischer makes to Cross. And yet, the lesson to take away from *Rushmore* is that the essential self is not immune from sexuality. To be certain, Valenzuela's attempt to theorize a pedagogy that might empower both teacher and student to confront and transform relations of oppression is not in question—indeed, this political ethic is the greatest strength of her work. In question is rather whether an authentic/aesthetic distinction can sustain such a project while avoiding the problems of sexual desire.

This brings us back to the issue of the cut that divides care from sexuality: can we create a safe distance by making a "cleaner" cut when demarcating the space of care? Lacan's concept of "*das Ding* [The Thing]," outlined in his seminar *The Ethics of Psychoanalysis*, may help answer this question. He uses the term *das Ding* to refer to the object cause of desire: "The whole progress of the subject is then oriented around the Ding as *Fremde*, strange and even hostile on occasion, or in any case the first outside. It is clearly a probing form of progress that seeks points of reference, but with relation to what?—with the world of desires" (*S* VII:52). His point is that the object that causes desire is not something familiar to us, something that we maintain a pleasant relationship with; rather, it is something strange [*Fremde*] to us. For example, take the standard psychoanalytic narrative of child development: what *causes* the child's desire for the object (the breast, the milk bottle, and so on) is the child's lack of the object itself, which is identified with displeasure (signaled by the child's cries). In this account, the child identifies the source of displeasure not with its real cause (the child's lack) but with an external agent, the one who takes the object of desire away. This primary relation to the object that causes desire ultimately leads us to identify the "strangeness" of our neighbors as the source of our displeasure insofar as we see this strangeness as a threat to our relation with our objects of desire. This "strangeness" in the other that we regard as threatening is das Ding. We should recognize that das Ding actually originates with us, with our lack of the object of desire. Stated differently, the strange object, or das Ding, is, as Lacan often put it, "us more than us"—it is our essential self.[22]

There is no guarantee that this essential self will not be something traumatic; in the case of care, this would be the very thing that dissolves the aesthetic/authentic boundary as well as the terms of care themselves: sexual desire. In fact, Lacan's view is that our essential self *is* traumatic. Specifically, he notes that das Ding is traumatic because the strangeness of our neighbors is, in the end, something *in us*. Returning to the issue of the cut, we cannot guard against trauma by insisting on a cleaner break because das Ding is produced precisely by the break (for instance, at the moment when the object was taken away from the child). Das Ding is the residual kernel that always upsets the balance of a break. We can never distill a purer form of care because there will never be the "cleanest break" from sexuality, and any break will create a leftover, a remainder, an "extimate object" (S VII:139)—that is, das Ding.

We should also point out another aspect of the pedagogy of care that remains problematic: namely, the aesthetic/authentic binary upon which it depends. If care is, as Valenzuela maintains, a relation of reciprocity, of connection, or of mutual respect, then it necessarily acts as a bridge between two people. As such, care is another name for a love that conceals the fundamental disjuncture separating the teacher and student. Though care theorists would argue that it is damaging to exclude love from pedagogy, would it not be equally damaging for love to serve only to mask a failed relation? What exactly is being compensated for when a connection of affect is made between two people? Could it not be the lack of any real teaching or learning? This possibility seems to exist in the aesthetic/authentic binary: authentic care might cover up for a lack of technical elements, such as knowledge, ideas, and other aspects important to learning, which concern aesthetic caring. Even more disturbing is the prospect that a teacher genuinely concerned with the types of oppression suffered by his or her students might, out of care for them, prevent the kind of critical thought that might produce an understanding of their oppression and its causes. Take the movie *School of Rock*, in which a substitute teacher, Dewey Finn, develops a caring relationship with his students.[23] Finn and his students come to care for one another, which climatically results in a jointly produced rock concert. Even though Finn truly cares for his students— demonstrated by many heart-to-heart talks in which Finn and his students share their deepest insecurities with one another, their "essential selves," if you will—it is not clear whether any knowledge was taught or learned throughout the movie. After all, the musical talents these students displayed in the rock concert were talents they already possessed.

Perhaps Lacan's logic of the signifier could shed some light on this potential danger: "A signifier is what represents the subject to another signifier."[24] Using the day/night dyad as an example, he shows that though "night" itself is not the opposite of day (the opposite of day is the absence of day), night does take on the status of day's opposite insofar as it "holds the place of" day's opposite.[25] The signifier (night) represents the subject (the absence of day) to another signifier (day). In this same away, the juxtaposition of aesthetic and authentic care is based upon an imaginary relation: aesthetic care only holds the place of authentic care's opposite, which, in reality, is the absence of care itself. If we focus solely on caring authentically, we lose the technical elements of aesthetic care. The danger is that the knowledge of oppressive relations could be lost as one of these aesthetic elements. Authentic care would only cover up the lack of learning and teaching of this knowledge, and, as a result, any sense of accomplishment or political solidarity would be empty. It seems to me that both aesthetic and authentic models should be equally insisted upon and that the true enemy is the absence of care itself.

V

The third stance of love in education is the technical position. On this view, the purpose of education is the transmission of knowledge, and the teacher's task is merely to transmit this knowledge as impartially as possible; therefore, love or any other affective dimension (including care) exceeds this task. In establishing content standards, the state has implicitly endorsed the technical position. The state claims that the impetus for adopting these standards was a void in education, in particular, the lack of any "specific vision of what students actually needed to know."[26] Standards fill this void by articulating the full scope of knowledge that education is to impart to students. With this void filled, educators must strive only to teach the specified knowledge to the best of their abilities. If love has the potential to distort the transmission of this knowledge, then it is no longer necessary.

Though the state's standards implicitly regard love as excessive, the state acknowledges that there is an appropriate space for love in pedagogy: it can be a tool for *motivating* students to acquire knowledge standards. In the technical position, even more clearly than in the pedagogies of eros and care, love serves no other purpose than to mask the lack of a teacher-student relation. For the state, the standards fully articulate knowledge. If the teacher fails to transfer this knowledge to the student, or if the student fails to acquire this knowledge, it is not because the standards themselves are flawed but because of a failure in the teacher-student relation. In such case, teachers are encouraged to utilize love, affect, care, and the like to bridge the disjunction so that they can effectively transfer the standards to the student. In becoming a mask for the disjunction in the teacher-student relation, love covers for the false construction of knowledge as standards. Here, the failure is not located within the standards-based knowledge as the thing mediating the teacher-student relation, nor is it an aspect of the relationship as such; rather, it is the failure of the teacher-student relationship to conform to an ideal—namely, the standards-based teaching relation.

The proponents of both erotic pedagogy and caring pedagogy have in mind the state's technical position, particularly its replication of state ideology, when they insist that love is necessary to inspire and embolden students to criticize and challenge the knowledge presented to them. But the logic of the technical position reveals something else about the relationship of love and knowledge, something other than the notion that love criticizes, or pokes holes in, knowledge. After all, for the state, love does not have an oppositional relationship with knowledge at all but, rather, a complementary one, one that mediates the passage of knowledge. Understood this way, love does not produce a lack in knowledge; it is an *effect* of a lack that already exists, the lack of a teacher-student relation. Furthermore, the technical position's claim that teacher-student relation is about hard-and-fast knowledge, and thus that love is excessive, can only be made if the completion of the teacher-student relationship coincides with the completion of knowledge. That is to say, by definition, love is excessive only if something is first posited as being complete. For the state, "completion" means acquiring the knowledge specified in the standards such that an ideal teacher-student relation is defined as the impartial, standards-based teaching relation.

So, the theorists of eros and care are correct when they insist that love is necessary to challenge the state-mandated standards, but for the opposite reason: love subverts the state's knowledge not because it stands in direct opposition to it but because its presence signifies a lack. A lack of what? A lack of a teacher-student relation, of course. This deals a heavy blow to the technical position: if love exists as an effect of a lack (as a supplement, in other words), then the lack in the teacher-student relation is a lack of knowledge. The need for love to motivate exists precisely because knowledge does not perfectly mediate the teacher-student relation—that is to say, the teacher-student relation defined as a relation of knowledge is still a failed relation. The implication is that standardization has not accomplished its task of fully articulating knowledge. Knowledge remains incomplete.

As we have just seen, the fundamental error of the technical position is that it sees love as something that *exceeds* the teacher-student relation. This position presupposes that love does not arise to supplement a lack but that love is simply external and unrelated to knowledge or to the teacher-student relation in general. This externality attributed to love is evident in how the technical position limits the relationship of love and knowledge to one of motivation—that is, for the technical position, love, like any other form of motivation, is just another way to aid the transmission of knowledge. But the pedagogies of eros and care also seem to assign love an external role, although this role is subversive in character: instead of aiding knowledge, love, from an external position, criticizes knowledge. But again, it is insofar as it is external to knowledge. Therefore, even though the exact function of love differs from position to position, the relation between love and knowledge is structurally similar for all three positions—love is consistently treated as external to knowledge.

At stake here is the precise location of knowledge's incompleteness. If love is external to knowledge, even its most critical powers are only capable of calling into question the particular content of knowledge, or, put another way, what is incomplete about knowledge is its particular content. We should not overlook that, instead of criticizing knowledge by holding that it represents a fundamental disjunction within the teacher-student relation (which knowledge does not fill), here love's criticism is that a particular content is missing from the standard order of knowledge, which, far from taking the fundamental disjunction into account, actually sustains the promise of wholeness by giving body to the gap as such. Hence, the frame of wholeness is sustained by directly representing a "missing part" that prevents the wholeness from becoming itself. Slavoj Zizek attributes this function to ideology, arguing that "this impossibility itself is distortedly represented-positivized within an ideological field—*that* is the role of ideological fantasy."[27] The trouble, then, is that love becomes synonymous with "ideological fantasy." Specifically, love becomes an external cover for the disjunction in the teacher-student relation by revealing knowledge to be inadequate for closing the gap and simultaneously "positivizing" the gap in another form.

VI

Love is an effect of a lack, as Lacan reminds. It is a supplement for the nonexistence of a relation, but this time love is not another name for a supplement for achieving the status of an ideal relation. "For," as he writes, "it is love that approaches being as such in the encounter." Here, love takes into account that a relationship of two people is structured around a void, that there is a fundamental disjunction separating the two, and that this void/separation prevents these two people from becoming whole, healed, one. Love is the truth that there is no such thing as an ideal relationship of wholeness. As Badiou observes, love "is a *production of truth*. The truth of what? That the Two, and not only the One, are at work in the situation."[28] True love, then, does not attempt to eradicate the truth of disjunction by constructing an imaginary cover—covers for which care, sex,

and knowledge are all names. Rather, true love sustains the truth
by sustaining the disjunction:

> The intelligence that love delivers is that the Two, as such,
> thought of as process, is neither stuck to the One which makes
> the difference opaque, nor detached from it to the point that one
> could count, like a third term, the interval which separates the
> components of it. Nor is it the Two which counts Two for One;
> nor is it the Two counted as One by the Three. It is an immanent
> construction of an indeterminate disjunction, which does not
> pre-exist it.[29]

Badiou's point is that love is not a method by which two disjunctive positions are reconciled and revealed to be similar
(imaginary identification), nor is it the name for a third space
that perfectly mediates the distance or gap between two people.
Instead, love structures the truth of the "Two," of the relation—
that there exists a disjunction such that the relation is always a
relation of two people.

For Badiou, as for Lacan, love does not describe an affective
emotion: love conceived in the imaginary register still retains an
affective dimension, but it is not an imagined construct linking
the two lovers together. Instead, love is the name for a radical
restructuring of a relation of two people—this is what Badiou
means when he calls love a "production of truth." Lovers, then,
are engaged subjects of love, living out the consequences of their
love, the consequences of life in this new relationship. In other
words, love is not affection, sexuality, or knowledge, but the
journey of a new collective subject—what Lacan calls "them-
two." It not only represents a new structure for two lovers but a
new collective vision of the world in which they live.

In the context of education, we can follow Lacan by saying that
love arises as a supplement for the truth that "there is no such
thing as a teacher-student relationship." Building on Badiou's
assertion that "what I will first reject is that, in love, each sex can
learn *about the other sex*," pedagogical love does not entail either
member seeking out some knowledge about the other, whether it
is the mysteries of their sexuality, their essential self, or anything

else. [30] This search for the other's knowledge in order to unlock the mystery of the other is what Badiou calls "counting the Two for One." Nor is the teacher-student relation perfectly mediated by knowledge (in the form of the state's standards), as the technical position holds. This use of knowledge as the missing link joining teacher and student is what Badiou calls "counting the Two as One by the Three." The implication here is something even more radical: pedagogical love does not entail the teacher transferring any knowledge (standards-based or otherwise) to the student, or vice versa. As Paulo Freire reminds us, "*Teaching cannot be a process of transference of knowledge from the one teaching to the learner*,"[31] for this gesture is again an attempt to erase the truth of their disjunction. In contrast, pedagogical love structures the truth that the teacher-student relation is a relation of Two.

In the love encounter, the teacher and student do not seek knowledge from or of each other, but, rather, they seek knowledge from the world *with* each other: "Knowledge emerges only through invention and re-invention human being pursue in the world, with the world, and with each other."[32] Love marks the splitting of the teacher-student relation that structures the truth of the void of the relation by pushing both parties into the world in the pursuit of knowledge: "Love is an enquiry of the world from the point of view of the Two, and not an enquiry of each term of the Two about the other."[33] Notice now that, with love, the incomplete status of knowledge is no longer a condition of its content but of its very frame: love means the pursuit of real knowledge, knowledge that is no longer limited to particular content passed from one to the other, but rather knowledge that can only be attained by each partner seeking it in the world. To put this differently, knowledge is by definition the inquiry we make of the world, which is a pursuit inaugurated by a loving encounter with a teacher. With love, education becomes an open space for thought from which emerges knowledge.

If education is to be a space where teacher and student search for knowledge, then we must strongly affirm that "yes, a teacher and student can and must love each other." But our previous discussion demonstrates that it is important to make clear that, when a teacher and student love one another, they do not have sex, they do not merely care for one another, nor do they pass knowledge between each other. Rather, with love, both teacher and student become self-aware and recognize that "there is no such thing as a teacher-student relationship." This truth opens a space for both lovers to preserve the distinctiveness of their positions by turning away from one another and toward the world in order to produce new knowledge through inquiry and thought. Let us not be mistaken: under the technical, rational conditions of standardization, the stakes are high. If education is to be a space of thought, we must insist with Freire that "it is impossible to teach without the courage to love."[34]

8

Teaching Abjection:
The Politics of Psychopedagogy

I

The post-9/11 culture has been a culture of fear, fostered by George W. Bush's "War on Terror," the Patriot Act and the curtailing of our civil liberties, the travesties at Abu Ghraib, and other embarrassments of executive power now too many to enumerate. The temptation is to take this culture of fear as the sign that our present historical situation is one that is marked by a continuous state of emergency—to be taken in the Carl Schmitt's sense of the exception to which the law applies precisely by not applying.[1] To be sure, this temptation is real, and as a testimony to its reality is the accompanying uproar of academics, critics, and media persons, both on the Left and the Right. Generally speaking, if these voices are not overtly encouraging us to consider our current existence as this state of emergency," then, at the very least, they call us to rethink the aims and goals of our current projects to reflect how such events have changed what is possible and necessary in the post-9/11 era. But against these rash announcements of the "new" status to which our times have become elevated is this clearheaded reminder given, some years ago, by Walter Benjamin in his "Theses on the Philosophy of History": "The tradition of the oppressed teaches us that the 'state of emergency' in which we live is not the exception but the rule."[2] This thesis—to be sure, a critique of Schmitt, the philosopher of the state of emergency par excellence, and of the paranoid, calls to consider Benjamin's own historical period as a new dispensation (this period was, of course, marked by Fascism, and perhaps there is another parallel to be drawn here, but I will not pursue it)—is a thesis that is still apropos of our current times.

What Benjamin's splash of sobriety reminds us today is of this reality: the marginality and threat with which we perceive ourselves to now be living is nothing new (that is, it is not an exception), rather, it has been (and this is the chief insight of oppressed people) the stuff with which life has always been composed. If we cannot see the everyday reality of the oppression that has only been made clear by recent events, then Benjamin's thesis rebukes our conception of history for being too weak to contain that concept; he continues:

> The current amazement that the things we are experiencing are "still" possible in the twentieth century is *not* philosophical. This amazement is not the beginning of knowledge—unless it is the knowledge that the view of history which gives rise to it is untenable.
>
> (257, original emphasis)

The conclusion to be drawn regarding the recent attention given to the notion that our time is the state of emergency is that concepts such as oppression, marginality, threat, violence, and so on are only real if they affect not simply the masses but also the academic and intellectual elite.

With his criticism of weak conceptions of history, Benjamin also offers this challenge: "We must attain to a conception of history that is in keeping with this insight. Then we shall clearly realize that it is our task to bring about a real state of emergency, and this will improve our position in the struggle against Fascism." The challenge, here, is true for us today as it was when Benjamin first wrote it: namely, we must think properly about our times with a concept of history that keeps fidelity with the everyday experiences of oppressed people from which an effective strategy against an oppressive political order might emerge.

The point, then, is not simply to ignore what conditions have been brought about by the "War on Terror" and Abu Ghraib, that is, in short, Bush's regime, nor is it to maintain a certain naiveté to the real changes it has brought; rather, the point is that we must put those events, their effects, as well as those who are affected, in their proper place within an enlarged historical framework that takes full account of oppression itself. What I will offer in this chapter is a move toward meeting Benjamin's challenge. I will first remind us of how education (at least, in the United States) already contains a minimum of exclusion within its structure and its self-conception, then I will connect this exclusionary logic to its material effects. It is within that context that I will address our current events. My thesis will be developed thus: by shifting focus onto the ways in which the "War on Terror" has affected the lives of everyday citizens, the desperate circumstances of those who are affected by the exclusionary logic of the U.S. educational apparatus has been forgotten. With such a shift, materially oppressed people are no longer simply oppressed anymore; rather, they have now become disavowed—that is, *abject*. I will, then, conclude by appropriating Benjamin's challenge for pedagogical theorizing and offer some initial gestures toward a "pedagogy of the abject"—that is, a pedagogy that maintains fidelity to the disavowed, repressed, and abjected oppressed.

II

The standardization process whose seeds were sown in the document "A Nation at Risk," begun some 20 years ago, and which has grown to maturity with the issuing of state curriculum content standards, is a process that takes places under the pretense that a more "academic" aim must be reasserted for public education.[3] The intentions driving the standardization movement are best stated by the California State Board of Education.[4] According to the California state board, what plagued public education was the emphasis placed upon the material needs of schools, such as updated textbooks, safe facilities, supplies, and the like. For the California state board, it is as if seeing these material needs met took away from what it considered the more crucial concern of deciding rigorous academic knowledge. Already the danger of this rhetoric of academics is visible: under the guise of concern for academics what will be forgotten is the reality of the oppressive material conditions certain students must endure at school. The solution proposed by the state of California, then, is to take direct control of deciding what this academic content will be, the result of which is, of course, the state curriculum content standards.

Though the impetus for devising these standards is the seemingly noble and disingenuously neutral cause of attaining a high level of academic excellence, the standardization initiatives are anything but noble or neutral. The notion of the "academic" is one that is ambiguous at best and is one that lends itself to be interrogated with such questions as "What defines the 'academic'?" "How do we know when something is 'academic'?" "Is the 'academic' something natural?" and so on. As Terry Eagleton has shown apropos of the notion of "literature," content that is considered part of categories of higher knowledge—such as the academic or the literary—occupy their position by socially and historically variable methods, and as such, those contents reflect the ideologies and relations of power that define the social groups that decide on such matters: "They [literature] refer in the end not simply to private taste, but to the assumptions by which certain social groups exercise and maintain power over others."[5] In short, the content that occupies the academic, to use Raymond Williams's words, is a "selective tradition."[6] Taking Eagleton's example, what we teach as the English literary canon does not enjoy its prestige by exuding some quality of "literariness" but, rather, by a long process of social and political power struggle.

Of course, the issue of academic knowledge/curriculum is not a new issue, and as I have already indicated above, I mean to rehearse these arguments only to remind us of the basic logic upon which the standardization movement is founded. It is Michael Apple who has already taken up this issue of, what he calls, a "politics of official knowledge."[7] There is not much more one could add to Apple's analyses. What I would like to bring into focus here is simply the exclusion that is necessary in order for the academic to become itself. If what we come to understand as academic only becomes so as a result of a selective or exclusion-ary process—a process that is loaded with political, ideological, and power implications and realities—then the silent unarticu-lated concomitant is the active *selection* of those contents that will stand in as the "unacademic," the academic's other.

This selection of academic's other is not another movement in itself but, simply, the other side of the academic selection pro-cess itself. For, the notion of the academic depends upon a binary logic: the academic is the positive term that relies on the presence of some negative term against which it can become meaningful. The clearest example of this intentionally chosen "unacademic" knowledge would be the California state board's own choice of labeling efforts to improve the material conditions of education. The state of California has *chosen* the issue of equitable material learning conditions as the unacademic concern against which the content standards appears as academic. Through its binary logic, the state is able to disavow the reality of material inequality.

Against the implication of the state's content standards, against its self-understanding as containing the academic proper, it must be emphasized that the oppositional relationship con-stituting this binary is not a natural but, rather, an imaginary relation. That is to say, there is no such thing as a natural aca-demic content or object. Something only becomes academic through the long-drawn-out process of selecting a tradition that Williams, Eagleton, and Apple have discussed. With his defini-tion of the signifier that I discussed in Chapter 7, "A signifier is what represents the subject to another subject," Jacques Lacan provides the formula in which to unravel the imaginary-based logic upon which binary constructions, such as the academic/other binary, are founded.[8] What Lacan means by this definition of the signifier is that the negative term in the binary is never the "true" opposite of the positive term; rather, it only "stands in" for the true opposite. To illustrate this formula, let us use one of Lacan's own examples, given in his seminar on *The Psychoses*.[9] Lacan argues that in the day/night binary, the negative term "night" is not the true opposite of day. Day's true opposite is none other than the absence of day itself. Unable to represent its absence to itself, day becomes sensible when night "stands in," or as Slavoj Zizek puts it, "holds the place of," day's opposite.[10] Or, to use Lacan's own vocabulary, night represents day's opposite to day. In the same way, for California, projects that address material inequalities only "hold the place of" curricular knowledge's negative. From this perspective, addressing material inequalities is not truly opposed to teaching curricular knowledge—the two are only imagined antipodes. Then, against California's logic, we should insist on how this situation is not an either/or situation—either pursue material improvements or knowledge—but rather, a both/and situation. The proper move here would be to remove the imaginary opposition and pursue both material improvements as well as knowledge, which is, as far as I understand it, the stance of many critical educators.

Formed with an imagined binary logic, there already exists a minimum of inequality at work in the structure of education in the United States. That is to say, someone's knowledge must always hold the place of the "unacademic."[11] This exclusion of other people's knowledge is explicitly stated in the California State Board's policy on standardization as it defends its overt bias toward Western civilizations, even suggesting Western knowledge as the natural and legitimate heritage of the United States. This obvious Eurocentrism is thus reflected in the standards: for example, under the topic of "tyrannies" and "illegitimate power," the standards lists, among others, Japan, Haiti, Latin America, as exemplars of the topic (Standards 12.9.4–5). What is most appalling about this claim and its reflection in the standards is the tone of certainty and self-transparency with which the board issues its opinions. Indeed this sense of naturalness is a rhetorical strategy through which the board legitimizes its biases.

III

This exclusion of others, which is an exclusion that reflects political power differentials, along race, class, gender, and national lines, is not an inequality that simply works on the level of content knowledge and debates over the academic. Rather, as I have implied by emphasizing the political implications at work in the constitution of content standards, this exclusion carries with it real material inequalities, the most obvious of which is making the neglect of material inequalities an official policy. Though the sphere of knowledge is not independent of the material base, in the same way, it is not completely determinative or determined by that base; rather, this sphere of knowledge is semiautonomous, and, for this reason, it is worth pursuing the connections between these two spheres.

First, it is clear that an ideological battle is being waged at the level of knowledge. Through the rhetoric of the academic, a particular kind of knowledge (which, by the board's own admission, is Eurocentric in character) is being legitimatized and taught while others are being delegitimized in the classroom. In order to give the school a critical name, we need go no further than the diagnosis Louis Althusser made apropos of the school within capitalist societies at large, and call the school an Ideological State Apparatus (ISA) for the way it reproduces social relations through the retransmission of a particular tradition of knowledge.[12] Moreover, we might even suggest that the school could only fully become an ISA with the aid of standardization, which, as we saw earlier, paved the way for the state to take direct control not simply of resource and budgetary matters but of the very organization and curriculum involved in public education.

The term standardization, in the U.S. context, does not mean only the standardization of curriculum but also the implementation of standardized high-stakes assessments and sanctions that accompany and enforce that curriculum. In simple terms, this means that there exists a putative measure for the state to take against those who might protest against the fact that their knowledge is not represented in the standards by resisting to adopt the official curriculum along with those who actively oppose the ideological imposition of U.S. hegemony in other ways.

Let us, for example, take the case of *Williams v. State of California*—the class action suit against the state of California for not providing adequate and equal conditions for education. In the complaint filed by the plaintiffs—who mostly live in the urban centers of California—one finds a long list of travesties that are given in order to typify the material inequalities of education in California. Such travesties include the daily presence of vermin and their feces, insufficient supply of books and materials, leaky buildings, and so on. According to the ideals set forth in the standardization initiatives, attentiveness to such gross inequalities is precisely what is ruining education and its purpose, which, for the board, is strictly the teaching of "academic" knowledge. The only course of action given to the people going to school under these conditions is to ignore the vermin infesting the building, "hunker down," absorb academic knowledge, and perform well on standardized tests, presumably schools will then qualify for the requisite federal funding to improve these conditions. To do otherwise would not only go against the state's official intention for education but can now be punished through the imposition of the sanctions set forth in the school accountability portion of the standardization initiative, which ultimately culminate in the school's take over by corporations or even the state itself. In other words, if teachers stray from the state standards and take school time to address the pressing matter of eradicating vermin and cleaning up rat feces, then those teachers are held accountable if test scores do not meet expectation. It is clear that rather than oblige the destiny that the state holds out, the plaintiffs of the Williams case are voicing the reality that the state and its attempts to regulate education have their limits. Moreover, we know that schools are not entities independent of their social and political contexts, which is indicated by the choice of the term "Ideological State Apparatus." What therefore concerns the people living in this context—namely, redress of the social wrong that is witnessed by the horrendous conditions in which the belonging schools exists—is simply made other and, on that basis, excluded by the concentration on academics.

What begins as a philosophical premise with an inherent inequality continues and manifests itself not only in the realm of ideology but in material reality itself. It is clear that the other marked and labeled by the state through its apparatus of standards is always-already oppressed, which becomes ever so clear with examples like the Williams case and countless others that go unpublicized. I take these realities to be what Benjamin was aiming at when he cited the "tradition of the oppressed."

IV

The hostage taking at a school in the southern Russian city of Beslan in 2004 was yet another unfortunate event added to the ever-growing list of tragedies that compose our historical moment. The question that was raised by news commentators, among other people, in the aftermath of this tragedy is this: how could a school, what is supposed to be a safe haven for children, become a target for terrorist action? In a weak attempt at situating this tragedy historically, various proprietors of spectacle (to use Guy Debord's critical term[13]) connected Beslan to the Columbine shootings that took place in the United States a few years earlier.[14] At work in this failed attempt to think historically is the complete forgetting that, for many people, Columbine and Beslan did not rob them of the belief that schools are safe havens because the conditions of school are already, and have been for some time, oppressive. This is in fact true for many of the students in urban centers, and it is not because of the supposed violence in the neighborhood, as so many Conservative commentators like to believe, but, precisely, because the state has allowed school conditions to become such (for example, the list of travesties in the Williams case, or the installation of prison-like conditions in those schools). The neglect of the state has allowed such atrocious conditions to exist.

Another case of this willful forgetting is, of course, Bush himself, who did not hesitate for one moment to exploit the Beslan tragedy for political gain as he quickly incorporated it into his personal "War on Terror." Bush took the opportunity to reemphasize that the "War on Terror" has named a new enemy, and with that naming a more pressing threat has supposedly emerged. What Bush forgets is how those who are answering his call to meet this new enemy by joining the military and his

"War on Terror" are doing so, in many cases, to escape the economic wasteland in which they live, which is something that
was dramatically documented by Michael Moore.[15] But neither should we think of Bush as the cause of all our problems.
Focusing exclusively on Bush is untrue because material inequality is a larger problem than Bush himself—in fact, it is part of the
system of capitalism. As a structural problem, we should refrain
from personalizing the contradictions of capitalism; we should
not displace those contradictions onto the person of Bush.
Keeping with Benjamin's challenge, how then can we resist the
temptation to think about Bush as the embodiment of contradiction, and how can we refrain from conceptualizing the events
that define his presidency as a dispensation in its own right?
The first lesson we must take away from the various methods of
sensationalizing and spectacularizing these tragedies would be to
understand how these events fall within a long history—indeed,
a tradition—of oppression on which our Global Order is founded.
Seen this way, it becomes clear that the structural and material
inequalities produced by capitalist globalization that oppress
many around the world is not an invention of Bush but, rather, is
something that was already set in motion well before Bush even
arrived on the scene. But more should be said on this topic.

Let us begin by returning to the binary logic upon which the
U.S. educational apparatus is grounded: if Lacan's diagnosis
of the imaginary structure of binaries is applied to Bush, then
what has been transformed is not this exclusionary binary logic
but rather the terms involved. Thus, by placing responses to the
"War on Terror" and its effect on our lives at the top of the agenda,
a new binary set has been put in place of the old academic/other
opposition: namely, the Cheney/Bush/Rove (CBR) fraternity on
one side and all who are affected globally by their policies on the
other. Since, as I am arguing, the frame of exclusion itself has not
been affected, what is no longer registered because of this reshuf-
fling is none other than oppression itself. This is because heavy
emphasis has been placed on how our lives are so irreparably
changed after 9/11, which obfuscates the truth that oppression
in the United States and worldwide has existed prior to 9/11 or

Bush's reign. We only need to call up the United States' history of imperial violence, which is reframed in the state standards as "the rise of the U.S. to its role as a world power" (Standard 11.4). But to further illustrate this repression of oppression, let us return to how the targeting of schools for violence was traced only as far back as Columbine, which fell out of the exploitative spectacularization of the Beslan tragedy. What is immediately lost in making Columbine the "first" Beslan is the long history of violence that has taken place in and around the area of many schools, usually in large urban centers and at the hands of the state. In fact, is this not the very point of the Williams case—that the state has failed to make its urban schools safe? Are not the plaintiffs suing for the very reason that the condition in which they attend school is so decrepit that it is a criminal act of state violence? Furthermore, it is unfortunate that as little attention the Williams case received, it is simply the only attention these students and schools have received at all, and as such, there goes unnoticed an even larger number of similar cases of state oppression in these schools, which, I attempted to argue, originates in the very constitutive logic of the state's educational agenda.

Julia Kristeva develops the concept that we can use to formulate the kind of disavowal that has characterized the destiny of the oppressed in our new times of war. In *Powers of Horror*, she writes:

> There looms, within abjection, one of those violent, dark revolts of being, directed against a threat that seems to emanate from an exorbitant outside or inside, ejected beyond the scope of the possible, the tolerable, the thinkable. It lies there, quite close, but it cannot be assimilated.[16]

This abject, then, is what is expunged from the very terms of intelligibility. The abject is not simply "the other," it is an other that undergoes a second order exclusion—the abject is, if you will, an other that is othered. There is no question that the CBR gang levied many devastating blows to the civil liberties of many mainstream Americans. To be sure, these effects must be contested. But to make Bush's policies and their effect on mainstream America the new exclusive terrain for debate and contestation, at the cost of neglecting capitalism as a whole, is to forget and disavow the "old" antagonism of material oppression for which the Williams case is a witness. In other words, in order for mainstream America to consider itself the oppressed as a result of Bush and his gang's policies, the materially oppressed themselves must be turned into an abject body and banished to the nether regions of political debate. The necessity for this abjection is clear: if we recenter political debates on the oppressive material conditions in which many children live and attend school (as the Williams case is attempting to do), then we risk sacrificing the opportunity to make central the tears in the social fabric that primarily affect mainstream America, and thus there is much jouissance in sustaining Bush, the "War on Terror," and their precipitating events, as the terrain of struggle.

The danger in sustaining this abject is as insidious as it is pressing: the radically negative turn that has taken place for the oppressed is nothing overt nor is it apparent in any obvious way; rather, it is a silent abjection, a quiet forgetting, whose real damage resides in the further obfuscation of the real issue at stake in our current times. To be clear, what this issue is, and this is the point to emphasize, is the struggle of the oppressed—a struggle that has been fought long before Bush and his "War on Terror;" an oppressed with whom Paulo Freire first challenged us to stand with in solidarity.[17] The lesson for critical educators would be to refrain from attacking any single figure and to examine the structural causes of material inequality while working with oppressed people to change the situation.

The cost for exceptionalizing the current historical moment is paid for by none other than the oppressed themselves. It is a cost that demands their moving from an already oppressive position as the other to the even more unintelligible and wretched location of the abject. In so doing, the danger that we are presented with is the danger of forgetting that the rectification of structural oppression and class antagonism is what is really at issue in phrases such as "social justice" and "freedom."

V

Developing the concept of the abject, Judith Butler offers the following statement: "I want to hold out for a conceptual apparatus that allows for the operation of abjection to have a kind of relative autonomy, even emptiness, contentlessness."[18] By describing the abject as a social position that is both excluded and contentless, it is remarkable how close Butler brings the concept of the abject to the philosophical thought of Jacques Ranciere—and so it is to him we now briefly turn.

In his remarkable book *Disagreement*, Ranciere reveals how the classic conception of democracy is constituted upon a fundamental miscount.[19] In the classical notion of democracy, only those who contribute a particular positive quality to the social order, such as riches or power, are counted as participants in that social order. For this reason, every democracy is predicated upon a miscount insofar as there always exists a part of society that has no particular positive qualities. This part of society is the "demos"—the people—which Ranciere describes, underlining their contentlessness, as the "part of no-part" or, simply, the "poor." With "poor," Ranciere does not refer to some empirical measure of poverty; rather, the poor, or the part of no-part, are those whom the dominant social paradigm considers to have no worth or interest. Because it has no interest of its own, the part of no-part, for Ranciere, does not stand for a particular set of interests (as do those who are counted by the social order) but, rather, the interests of the people, the demos, and therefore they represent the interest of the entire social body:

> For freedom—which is merely the position of those who have absolutely no other, no merit, no wealth—is counted at the same time as being common virtue. It allows the demos (that is, the actual gathering of men of no position, these men whom Aristotle tell us "had no part in anything") to identify with the whole of the community through homonymy.[20]

Could we not say this same thing about the abject? Are the abject not the part of no-part? The abject is not counted in the logic of social order, it remains outside, but, at the same time, the abject, as Butler argues, has no content of itself; it is a formally empty position. This would mean that far from fighting on behalf of civilization, those who claim they criticize Bush and his political agenda simply represent the particular interests of those who are counted by our political order. Opposed to this claim is the claim of the abject. By contrast, the abject—void of any particular interest insofar as they disavowed from the social order all together—stand for the interest of the whole social body. Before we state what the abject's claim actually is, we must unfold Ranciere's thought a bit more.

For Ranciere, the founding political act then takes place when this part of no-part speaks and articulates the wrong of the miscount. Against solipsistic claims that any body that is an abject body necessarily is absent of any agency and subjectivity (indeed, Kristeva speaks of the abject as containing an explosive potential agency) and against any claims to the necessity for a political vanguard, Ranciere gives the formal structure to politics that begins with the poor themselves speaking. The radicality of the poor's act is that in so speaking, they already elevate themselves to the same level as those who count within society—the part of no-part, as Ranciere puts it, presupposes the equality of speaking beings. For Ranciere, what is radical in the very act of speaking and articulating the wrong is that the part of no-part presupposes that they can be heard and understood, and, in this way, they become the place of universal freedom.

What Ranciere develops in *Disagreement* is not merely theoretical in any way; after all, is this not the radical step that the abject of our times already accomplished? The Williams case, here, is the exemplar. First, the plaintiffs of the Williams case are speaking against the inherent inequality of education in the United States—that they are not counted in the formation of education. The plaintiffs, without representing a particular interest of their own, demand an egalitarian-universal demand—namely, the demand for an equal education for all. Because the complaint of the plaintiffs is understood by those whose interest is included in the community, the plaintiff's equality with those people is presupposed.

What the plaintiffs accomplished is nothing less than what Alain Badiou would describe as an event.[21] An event is, for Badiou, addressed universally, and as such the egalitarian demand for which the plaintiffs stand is not simply their own possession but is addressed universally and therefore open to all. Or, to place this within Ranciere's language, the egalitarian demand of the part of no-part, or what I am calling the abject, which in the case of the plaintiffs is the egalitarian demand for an equal education for all, is not a representation of the interests of a particular part of society but of the entire social body as such. All are entitled to an equal education. The turn that is suggested by placing this event within Badiou's and Ranciere's terms is that the question, "What must be done?" which we asked above, has already been answered by the abject themselves, and that answer is this: we must make the radical decision to stand in solidarity with the oppressed as they make their egalitarian demands and fight through the precipitant struggle. Against the old worries of acting as vanguards and imposing our interests upon the abject, the abject have, themselves, turned the tables: it is not us who are attempting to "interpellate" the oppressed, but rather, they who are attempting to "interpellate" us. In order to make this stance with the abject, it is clear that we must first abandon the tactics of forefronting how the Bush regime made life difficult and reassert, instead, how the issues at stake, which is the very issue that gives shape to the social terrain that we inhabit, is oppression itself.

Two words of caution. First, I do not want to be misconstrued as romanticizing the Williams case or the oppressed. The intention here is to think about how recent events have transformed the terrain of struggle and, in response, to think clearly as to how we might proceed. It is also to remind how the causes that address a certain segment of society are not merely those that affect that segment alone but are also the ones that affect the entire social body by way of the abject part of no-part. Second, as Badiou reminds us, any event can be betrayed.[22] That is to say, apropos of the Williams case, the egalitarian demand for an equal education for all can be forsaken by settling before real equality is achieved. The only real way to satisfy the abject's demand should be to restructure society in order to actualize equal material educational conditions in the real, and we must settle for nothing less.

What, then, is a "pedagogy of the abject"? Differing from the traditional notions of pedagogy as a method of teaching, I wish to assert that a pedagogy of the abject would be a method of thinking with the abject about how to act according to the egalitarian demand that they have articulated (to remind us once again, it is the demand for radical equality). Or, to put this in more Badiouian terms, this pedagogy would be a procedure of fidelity to the event of the abject speaking. This pedagogy would be thinking through how we must act and think in our current situation according to the event. Using the terms of Chapter 6, the pedagogy of the abject is the pedagogy of truth. Thus the task placed before critical educators is precisely to think with the abject how to transform the situation in order to see to it that all people receive an equal education. Indeed, this would necessitate, at the very least, a revolutionary act of some kind (the task is to develop what this act might be). The ultimate goal for this pedagogy would be to meet Benjamin's challenge of bringing about a real state of emergency, one that will be the strongest weapon against (and, here, I do, after all, draw the last parallel with Benjamin's thesis) the fascisms of our time.

Notes

Introduction

1. Sigmund Freud, "Preface to Aichhorn's *Wayward Youth*," in *The Standard Edition of the Complete Psychological Works of Sigmund Freud*, ed. and trans. James Strachey, 24 vols. (London: Hogarth, 1953–74), 16:273. All references to the *Standard Edition* will hereafter be made with the abbreviation *SE* followed by volume and page numbers.
2. *SE* 16:273, original emphasis. Freud makes a similar statement in one of his final theoretical papers, "Analysis Terminable and Interminable." "It almost looks," he writes, "as if analysis were the third of those 'impossible' professions in which one can be sure beforehand of achieving unsatisfying results. The other two, which have been known much longer, are education and government," *SE* 23:248.
3. *SE* 16:273.
4. *SE* 22:146.
5. See Anna Freud, *Psychoanalysis for Teachers and Parents* (New York: W. W. Norton, 1979).
6. *SE* 22:149.
7. *SE* 22:150.
8. *SE* 22:146.
9. Of course, I do not claim that this book is singular in its aims. Rather, I more modestly claim that it follows and continues a path already blazed by "so many capable workers." Some of these are Douglas Aoki, "The Thing Never Speaks for Itself: Lacan and the Pedagogical Politics of Clarity," *Harvard Educational Review* 70, no. 3 (2000); Stephen Appel, *Positioning Subjects: Psychoanalysis and Critical Educational Studies* (Westport, CT: Bergin and Garvey, 1996); Charles Bingham, *Authority Is Relational: Rethinking Educational Empowerment* (Albany: SUNY Press, 2008); Mark Bracher, *Radical Pedagogy: Identity, Generativity, and Social*

Transformation (New York: Palgrave Macmillan, 2006); Mark Bracher, *The Writing Cure: Psychoanalysis, Composition, and the Aims of Education* (Carbondale and Edwardsville: Southern Illinois University Press, 1999); Deborah Britzman, *After-Education: Anna Freud, Melanie Klein, and Psychoanalytic Histories of Learning* (Albany: SUNY Press, 2003); Deborah Britzman, *Lost Subjects, Contested Objects: Toward a Psychoanalytic Inquiry of Learning* (Albany: SUNY Press, 1998); Deborah Britzman, *Novel Education: Psychoanalytic Studies of Learning and Not Learning* (New York and Frankfurt: Peter Lang, 2006); Elizabeth Ellsworth, *Teaching Positions: Difference, Pedagogy, and the Power of Address* (New York: Teachers College Press, 1997); Shoshana Felman, "Education and Crisis, or the Vicissitudes of Teaching," *American Imago* 48, no. 1 (1991); Shoshana Felman, "Psychoanalysis and Education: Teaching Terminable and Interminable," *Yale French Studies* 63 (1982); Joe L. Kincheloe and William F. Pinar, eds., *Curriculum as Social Psychoanalysis: The Significance of Place* (Albany: SUNY Press, 1991); Mick Markham, "Through the Looking Glass: Reflective Teaching through a Lacanian Lens," *Curriculum Inquiry* 29, no. 1 (1999); Alice Pitt, *The Play of the Personal: Psychoanalytic Narratives of Feminist Education* (New York and Frankfurt: Peter Lang, 2003); Donyell Roseboro, *Jacques Lacan and Education: A Critical Introduction* (Rotterdam: Sense, 2008); Robert Samuels, *Teaching the Rhetoric of Resistance: The Popular Holocaust and Social Change in a Post 9/11 World* (New York: Palgrave Macmillan, 2007); Sharon Todd, *Learning from the Other: Levinas, Psychoanalysis, and Ethical Possibilities in Education* (Albany: SUNY Press, 2003); as well as the edited collections jan jagodzinski, ed., *Pedagogical Desire: Authority, Seduction, Transference, and the Question of Ethics* (Westport, CT: Bergin and Garvey, 2002); Alice Pitt, Judith P. Robertson, and Sharon Todd, eds., *Special Issue on Psychoanalysis*, Vol. 14, *Jct: Journal of Curriculum Theorizing* (1998); Sharon Todd, ed., *Learning Desire: Perspectives on Pedagogy, Culture, and the Unsaid* (New York: Routledge, 1997).

10. Felman makes a similar claim: "Psychoanalysis is thus a pedagogical experience: as a process which gives access to new knowledge hitherto denied to consciousness, it affords what might be called a lesson in cognition (and in miscognition), an epistemological instruction" ("Psychoanalysis and Education," 27).

11. For helpful guides through Lacan's discourse, see Suzanne Barnard and Bruce Fink, eds., *Reading Seminar XX: Lacan's Major Work*

on Love, Knowledge, and Feminine Sexuality (Albany: SUNY Press, 2002); Justin Clemens and Russell Grigg, eds., *Jacques Lacan and the Other Side of Psychoanalysis: Reflections on Seminar XVII* (Durham, NC: Duke University Press, 2006); Bruce Fink, *A Clinical Introduction to Lacanian Psychoanalysis* (Cambidge, MA: Harvard University Press, 1997); Bruce Fink, *The Lacanian Subject* (Princeton, NJ: Princeton University Press, 1995); Bruce Fink, Maire Jaanus, and Richard Feldstein, eds., *Reading Seminar I and II: Lacan's Return to Freud* (Albany: SUNY Press, 1996); Bruce Fink, Maire Jaanus, and Richard Feldstein, eds., *Reading Seminar XI: Lacan's Four Fundamental Concepts of Psychoanalysis* (Albany: SUNY Press, 1995); Slavoj Zizek, *The Sublime Object of Ideology* (New York: Verso, 1989); Slavoj Zizek, ed., *Cogito and the Unconscious* (Durham, NC: Duke University Press, 1998).

12. Jacques Lacan, *Écrits: The First Complete Edition in English*, trans. Bruce Fink (New York: W. W. Norton, 2007).

13. See *SE* 4 and 5.

14. In this regard, jan jagodzinski deserves special commendation for his faithful work on Lacan in educational studies; see his "Youth Culture" trilogy, jan jagodzinski, *Music in Youth Culture: A Lacanian Approach* (New York: Palgrave Macmillan, 2005); jan jagodzinski, *Television and Youth Culture: Televised Paranoia* (New York: Palgrave Macmillan, 2008); and jan jagodzinski, *Youth Fantasies: The Perverse Landscape of the Media* (New York: Palgrave Macmillan, 2004).

Chapter 1

1. Sigmund Freud and Josef Breuer, *Studies in Hysteria*, trans. Nicola Luckhurst (New York and London: Penguin, 2004), 111.

2. Recently, there has been a renewed interest in trauma; see, for example, Cathy Caruth, *Unclaimed Experience: Trauma, Narrative and History* (Baltimore and London: Johns Hopkins University Press, 1996); Shoshana Felman and Dori Laub, *Testimony: Crises of Witnessing in Literature, Psychoanalysis, and History* (New York and London: Routledge, 1992); Dominick LaCapra, *History and Memory after Auschwitz* (Ithaca, NY: Cornell University Press, 1998); Dominick LaCapra, *Writing History, Writing Trauma* (Baltimore and London: Johns Hopkins University Press, 2000); Ruth Leys, *Trauma: A Genealogy* (Chicago: Chicago University Press, 2000);

Michael Rothberg, *Traumatic Realism: The Demands of Holocaust Representation* (Minneapolis: University of Minnesota Press, 2000). For a particularly revealing study of trauma, see Paul Eisenstein, *Traumatic Encounters: Holocaust Representation and the Hegelian Subject* (Albany: SUNY Press, 2003). See also the collection, Cathy Caruth, ed., *Trauma: Explorations in Memory* (Baltimore and London: Johns Hopkins University Press, 1995). For trauma in education studies, see Shoshana Felman, "Education and Crisis, or the Vicissitudes of Teaching," *American Imago* 48, no. 1 (1991); Marla Morris, *Curriculum and the Holocaust: Competing Sites of Memory and Representation* (New York: Lawrence Erlbaum, 2001).

3. The emphasis on trauma made here should not be taken as a criticism of Deborah Britzman's provocative and important concept of "difficult knowledge," see Deborah Britzman, *Lost Subjects, Contested Objects: Toward a Psychoanalytic Inquiry of Learning* (Albany: SUNY Press, 1998), especially, Chapter 6. That said, there are important differences between the two: whereas "difficult" refers to the content of knowledge, "trauma," on my account, always refers to the relation between knowledge and the individual.

4. For a helpful discussion on the implications of the unconscious on the philosophy of consciousness, see Slavoj Zizek, ed., *Cogito and the Unconscious* (Durham, NC: Duke University Press, 1998).

5. Sigmund Freud, "The Unconscious," in *The Standard Edition of the Complete Psychological Works of Sigmund Freud*, ed. and trans. James Strachey, 24 vols. (London: Hogarth, 1953–74), 14:172.

6. Sigmund Freud, *The "Wolfman" and Other Cases*, in *The New Penguin Freud*, ed. Adam Phillips, trans. Louise Adey Huish (New York: Penguin, 2003), 134.

7. Jacques Lacan, *The Seminar of Jacques Lacan, Book VII: The Ethics of Psychoanalysis*, trans. Dennis Porter (New York: Norton, 1992), 61.

8. Eric Laurent, "Alienation and Separation (I)," in *Reading Seminar XI: Lacan's Four Fundamental Concepts of Psychoanalysis*, ed. Richard Feldstein, Bruce Fink, and Maire Jaanus (Albany: SUNY Press, 1995), 27.

9. Jacques Lacan, "The Subversion of the Subject and the Dialectic of Desire in the Freudian Unconscious," in *Écrits: A Selection* (New York and London: W. W. Norton, 2004), 286.

10. Christopher Nolan and Jonathan Nolan, *Memento*, ed. Christopher Nolan (Sony Pictures, 2000).

11. Slavoj Zizek, *For They Know Not What They Do: Enjoyment as a Political Factor*, 2nd ed. (London: Verso, 2002), 2, original emphasis.

Chapter 2

1. John Stuart Mill, *On Liberty* (Arlington Heights, IL: AHM, 1947), 28.

2. Sigmund Freud and Josef Breuer, *Studies in Hysteria*, trans. Nicola Luckhurst (New York and London: Penguin, 2004), 81.

3. Karl Marx, *Capital*, trans. Ben Fowkes, vol. 1 (New York: Penguin, 1990), 104.

4. Jacques Lacan, *The Seminar of Jacques Lacan, Book I: Freud's Papers on Technique, 1953–1954*, trans. John Forrester (New York: W. W. Norton, 1988), 85.

5. It should be mentioned that the clinic is for Lacan, and Freud as well, always a model of social relations at large.

6. Sigmund Freud, *The "Wolfman" and Other Cases*, in *The New Penguin Freud*, ed. Adam Phillips, trans. Louise Adey Huish (New York: Penguin, 2003), 143.

7. Sigmund Freud, *Introductory Lectures on Psycho-Analysis*, in *The Standard Edition of the Complete Psychological Works of Sigmund Freud*, ed. and trans. James Strachey, 24 vols. (London: Hogarth, 1953–74), 16: 286.

8. Sigmund Freud, *Dora: An Analysis of a Case of Hysteria* (New York: Touchstone, 1963), 7.

9. Jacques Lacan, "The Mirror Stage as Formative of the Function of the I," in *Écrits: A Selection* (New York and London: W. W. Norton, 2004).

10. Freud defines identification thus: "We can only see that identification endeavors to mould a person's own ego after the fashion of the one that has been taken as a model." Sigmund Freud, *Group Psychology and the Analysis of the Ego* (New York: W. W. Norton, 1959), 48.

11. Jacques Lacan, "The Subversion of the Subject and the Dialectic of Desire in the Freudian Unconscious," in *Écrits: A Selection* (New York and London: W. W. Norton, 2004), 294.

Chapter 3

1. Sigmund Freud, *Papers on Technique*, in *The Standard Edition of the Complete Psychological Works of Sigmund Freud*, ed. and trans. James Strachey, 24 vols. (London: Hogarth, 1953–1974), vol. 12.

2. Jacques Lacan, *The Seminar of Jacques Lacan, Book I: Freud's Papers on Technique, 1953–1954*, trans. John Forrester (New York: W. W. Norton, 1988).

3. Jacques Lacan, *The Seminar of Jacques Lacan, Book XVII: The Other Side of Psychoanalysis*, trans. Russell Grigg (New York: W. W. Norton, 2007). For helpful commentary on Lacan's four discourses, see Justin Clemens and Russell Grigg, eds., *Jacques Lacan and the Other Side of Psychoanalysis: Reflections on Seminar XVII* (Durham, NC: Duke University Press, 2006); Bruce Fink, *The Lacanian Subject* (Princeton, NJ: Princeton University Press, 1995), chap. 9; Slavoj Zizek, *Iraq: The Borrowed Kettle* (New York and London: Verso, 2005).
4. Pierre Boileau and Thomas Narcejac, "Vertigo," ed. Alfred Hitchcock (Universal Studios, 1958).
5. Fink, *Lacanian Subject*, 89.
6. Sigmund Freud, *Group Psychology and the Analysis of the Ego* (New York: Norton, 1959), 46.
7. Jacques Ranciere, *The Ignorant Schoolmaster: Five Lessons in Intellectual Emancipation*, trans. Kristin Ross (Stanford, CA: Stanford University Press, 1991).
8. The title of Chapter 1.

Chapter 4

1. For the most insightful account of trauma, in the context of Holocaust studies, see Paul Eisenstein, *Traumatic Encounters: Holocaust Representation and the Hegelian Subject* (Albany: SUNY Press, 2003).
2. Karl Marx, *Capital*, trans. Ben Fowkes, vol. 1 (New York: Penguin, 1990), 799.
3. We must recognize the many criticisms that have been made of psychoanalysis. Regretfully, space only permits us to focus on a productive discussion of psychoanalysis, and therefore we will not be engaging these positions. For a sampling of the positions at stake in this work, see Toril Moi, "From Femininity to Finitude: Freud, Lacan, and Feminism, Again," *Signs: Journal of Women in Culture and Society* 29, no. 3 (2004).
4. Rene Descartes, *Meditations on First Philosophy*, trans. John Cottingham (Cambridge and New York: Cambridge University Press, 1986).
5. John Dewey, *Democracy and Education* (New York: Free Press, 1997); Paulo Freire, *Pedagogy of the Oppressed*, trans. Myra Bergman Ramos (New York and London: Continuum, 1970).
6. Freire, *Pedagogy of the Oppressed*, 79.

7. Karl Marx, "Wage Labour and Capital," in *The Marx-Engels Reader*, ed. Robert C. Tucker (New York: W. W. Norton, 1978), 214, original emphasis.

8. It is, of course, Lacan who refers to psychoanalysis as the "other side" of Enlightenment philosophy, see Jacques Lacan, *The Seminar of Jacques Lacan, Book XVII: The Other Side of Psychoanalysis*, trans. Russell Grigg (New York: W. W. Norton, 2007).

9. In James Strachey's translation, it is: "Where id was, there ego shall be." Sigmund Freud, *The Standard Edition of the Complete Psychological Works of Sigmund Freud*, ed. and trans. James Strachey, 24 vols. (London: Hogarth, 1953–74), 22: 80.

10. Deleuze and Foucault are usually put at the center of this "de-centering," see Gilles Deleuze and Felix Guattari, *Anti-Oedipus: Capitalism and Schizophrenia* (Minneapolis: Minnesota University Press, 1983); Michel Foucault, *Order of Things: An Archaeology of the Human Sciences* (New York: Routledge, 2001).

11. Jacques Lacan, "The Mirror Stage as Formative of the Function of the I," in *Écrits: A Selection* (New York and London: W. W. Norton, 2004), 3.

12. Jacques Lacan, *The Seminar of Jacques Lacan, Book XI: The Four Fundamental Concepts of Psychoanalysis*, ed. Jacques-Alain Miller, trans. Alan Sheridan (New York and London: W. W. Norton, 1981).

13. Lacan, "Mirror Stage as Formative of the Function of the I," 4.

14. Sigmund Freud and Josef Breuer, *Studies in Hysteria*, trans. Nicola Luckhurst (New York and London: Penguin, 2004).

15. Sigmund Freud, *The "Wolfman" and Other Cases*, in *The New Penguin Freud*, ed. Adam Phillips, trans. Louise Adey Huish (New York: Penguin, 2003), 134. Original emphasis.

16. Lacan states this thesis numerous times throughout much of his work; see, for example, Lacan, *S XI*, 131.

17. These are, of course, references to Freud's three great works on dreams, jokes, and psychopathology.

18. It is indeed unfortunate when one sees a theorist embarrass himself by evoking psychoanalysis—specifically, the unconscious—in order to describe something that always evades symbolization—it is enough to recall again that Lacan's formula is that "the unconscious is the discourse of the Other."

19. Sigmund Freud, *The Psychopathology of Everyday Life*, trans. James Strachey (New York and London: W. W. Norton, 1965), 102–3.

20. Georg Lukacs, *History and Class Consciousness* (Cambridge, MA: MIT Press, 1968).

21. Karl Marx, "Class Struggle and Mode of Production," in *The Marx-Engels Reader*, ed. Robert C. Tucker (New York and London: W. W. Norton, 1978), 192–93.

22. Louis Althusser famously uses Lacan's theory of the mirror stage as the model for his theory of ideology. However, there are important differences between Althusser's theory of ideological interpellation and Lacan's theory of the mirror-relation. For an account of these differences, see Mladen Dolar, "Beyond Interpellation," *Qui Parle* 6, no. 2, Spring/Summer (1993).

23. The *a* is an abbreviation for "*autre*"—the French word for "other." It indicates the otherness of the object.

24. Slavoj Zizek suggestively develops the psychoanalytic concept of fundamental fantasy into a theory of ideology, see Slavoj Zizek, *The Sublime Object of Ideology* (New York: Verso, 1989).

25. Sigmund Freud, *The Uncanny*, trans. Hugh Haughton (New York: Penguin, 2003).

26. Zizek gives another example of failed recognition: a woman, living in a heavily bureaucratic society, receives notice from the bureaucracy that her identification card is missing. In reality the woman's card is not missing and is in her possession. To clear up the matter, the woman goes to the state bureaucracy and shows the card to the clerk. The bureaucrat responds that according to the records the woman's card is "officially" missing, thus the one in her possession is invalid, technically "missing." What Zizek's anecdote finely illustrates is the bureaucracy's failure to recognize the woman as identical to the identification card. Slavoj Zizek, *Revolution at the Gates: Zizek on Lenin, the 1917 Writings* (New York and London: Verso, 2002), 185.

27. Jacques Lacan, "The Instance of the Letter in the Unconscious, or Reason since Freud," in *Écrits: A Selection* (New York and London: W. W. Norton, 2002), 157.

Chapter 5

1. Some foundational texts are Paulo Freire, *Pedagogy of the Oppressed*, trans. Myra Bergman Ramos (New York and London: Continuum, 1970); Henry Giroux, *Theory and Resistance in Education: Towards a Pedagogy for the Opposition* (Westport, CT: Bergin and Garvey, 1983);

Peter McLaren, *Life in Schools: An Introduction to Critical Pedagogy in the Foundations of Education* (Needham Heights, MA: Allyn and Bacon, 1998).

2. See also Paulo Freire, "The Adult Literacy Process as Cultural Action for Freedom," *Harvard Educational Review* 68, no. 4 (1998); Paulo Freire, "Cultural Action for Freedom," *Harvard Educational Review* 68, no. 4 (1998); Paulo Freire, *Pedagogy of Freedom: Ethics, Democracy, and Civic Courage,* trans. Patrick Clarke (Lanham, MD: Rowman and Littlefield, 1998); Paulo Freire, *The Politics of Education: Culture, Power and Liberation* (Westport, CT: Bergin and Garvey, 1984).

3. Freire, "Adult Literacy Process," 485.

4. Elizabeth Ellsworth, "Why Doesn't This Feel Empowering? Working through the Repressive Myth of Critical Pedagogy," *Harvard Educational Review* 59, no. 3 (1989).

5. Much of this debate was played out in the following publications: Henry Giroux, *Border Crossings: Cultural Workers and the Politics of Education* (New York and London: Routledge, 2005); Henry Giroux and Patrick Shannon, eds., *Education and Cultural Studies: Toward a Performative Practice* (New York and London: Routledge, 1997); Patti Lather, "Critical Pedagogy and Its Complicities: A Praxis of Stuck Places," *Educational Theory* 48, no. 4 (1998); Carmen Luke and Jennifer Gore, eds., *Feminisms and Critical Pedagogy* (New York and London: Routledge, 1992); Peter McLaren, *Critical Pedagogy and Predatory Culture* (New York and London: Routledge, 1995).

6. Charles Bingham refers to this silent citation as Freire's "debt"; see Charles Bingham, "On Paulo Freire's Debt to Psychoanalysis: Authority on the Side of Freedom," *Studies in Philosophy and Education* 21 (2002).

7. It should be mentioned that the need for psychoanalysis would not surprise Ellsworth as she is well versed in psychoanalysis; see Elizabeth Ellsworth, *Teaching Positions: Difference, Pedagogy, and the Power of Address* (New York: Teachers College Press, 1997).

8. Jacques Lacan, *The Seminar of Jacques Lacan, Book XI: The Four Fundamental Concepts of Psychoanalysis,* ed. Jacques-Alain Miller, trans. Alan Sheridan (New York and London: W. W. Norton, 1981), 131.

9. Jacques Lacan, "The Subversion of the Subject and the Dialectic of Desire in the Freudian Unconscious," in *Écrits: A Selection* (New York and London: W. W. Norton, 2004), 293.

10. Slavoj Zizek, *The Sublime Object of Ideology* (New York: Verso, 1989), 19.
11. Slavoj Zizek, *Did Somebody Say Totalitarianism? Five Interventions in the (Mis)Use of a Notion* (New York: Verso, 2002), 141.
12. Sigmund Freud, "Repression," in *The Standard Edition of the Complete Psychological Works of Sigmund Freud*, ed. James Strachey, trans. James Strachey, 24 vols. (London: Hogarth, 1953–74), 14: 147.
13. Paulo Freire, *Pedagogy of Hope* (New York: Continuum, 2003), 44.
14. Sigmund Freud, *The "Wolfman" and Other Cases*, in *The New Penguin Freud*, ed. Adam Phillips, trans. Louise Adey Huish (New York: Penguin, 2003).

Chapter 6

1. Jacques Lacan, The Seminar of Jacques Lacan, Book XVII: The Other Side of Psychoanalysis, trans. Russell Grigg (New York: W. W. Norton, 2007), 109.
2. Jacques Lacan, "Science and Truth," Newsletter of the Freudian Field 3 (1989): 19.
3. Alain Badiou, Ethics: An Essay on the Understanding of Evil (New York: Verso, 2002). Hereafter, cited as Ethics in the text.
4. Alain Badiou, Infinite Thought: Truth and the Return of Philosophy, trans. Justin Clemens and Oliver Feltham (New York: Continuum, 2003), 61.
5. Alain Badiou, "Art and Philosophy," lacanian ink 17, (Fall 2000): 61.
6. For a full account of Badiou's philosophical project, see Peter Hallward, Badiou: A Subject to Truth (Minneapolis: University of Minnesota Press, 2003).
7. See Gilles Deleuze and Felix Guattari, A Thousand Plateaus (Minneapolis: University of Minnesota Press, 1987).
8. See Jean-Paul Sartre, Critique of Dialectical Reason, Volume 1, trans. Alan Sheridan-Smith (New York and London: Verso, 2004).
9. See also Alain Badiou, "The Scene of Two," lacanian ink 21, (Spring/Summer 2003); Alain Badiou, "What Is Love?" Umbr(a) 1 (1996). For how a Badiouian theory of love pertains to an educational context, see Chapter 7.
10. See Louis Althusser, The Humanist Controversy and Other Texts, trans. Francois Matherson and G. M. Goshgarian (New York and London: Verso, 2003).

11. See Louis Althusser, "Ideology and Ideological State Apparatus," in Lenin and Philosophy and Other Essays (New York: Monthly Review Press, 2001).
12. Badiou, "Art and Philosophy," 67.
13. Elsewhere, Tyson Lewis and I explore this notion of the "pedagogy of the event;" see our Daniel Cho and Tyson Lewis, "Education and Event: Thinking Radical Pedagogy in an Era of Standardization," Simile: Studies in Media & Information Literacy Education 5, no. 2 (2005).
14. See, again, ibid.
15. See, again, Chapter 7.
16. Alain Badiou, "On the Philosophy of the Open" (lecture, University of California, Los Angeles, 12/11/03 2003).

Chapter 7

1. For another analysis of teacher-student sex and the discourse of sexual harassment, see Benjamin Baez, "Sex Harassment in Schools: The Politics of Law, Power, Sexuality, and Speech," *Educational Theory* 51, no. 1 (2001). I will say more on the position Baez takes below in my discussion of, what I will call, the "erotic position."
2. Donna Huffaker, "Teacher Pleads Not Guilty in Sex Case: Judge Rejects Bid to Lower Granda Hills High Instructor's Bail," *Daily News of Los Angeles,* March 17, 1999.
3. Lisa Weiss and Donna Huffaker, "Teacher Held as Suspect in Teen Sex Case," *Daily News of Los Angeles,* March 15, 1999.
4. A. Payne, "Election" (Los Angeles: Paramount, 1999).
5. For another analysis of love as distinct from sexuality, see Anna Kornbluh, "For the Love of Money," *Historical Materialism* 10, no. 4 (2002).
6. Jacques Lacan, *The Seminar of Jacques Lacan, Book XX: Encore: On Feminine Sexuality, the Limits of Love and Knowledge*, trans. Bruce Fink (New York: W. W. Norton, 1988).
7. Alain Badiou, "What Is Love?" *Umbr(a)* One (1996): 49.
8. Alain Badiou, "On Love" (seminar presented at the University of California, Los Angeles, May 2004).
9. Though, here, the term "eros" is used in somewhat similar ways as Plato—with whom eros is often associated with—it is also used

in a manner that is distinct from Plato. For discussions that deal directly with Plato and eros, see Kal Alston, "Teaching, Philosophy, and *Eros*: Love as a Relation to Truth," *Educational Theory* 41, no. 4 (1991); Timothy Simpson and James Scott Johnston, "*Eros* between Plato and Garrison: Recovering Lost Desire," *Educational Theory* 52, no. 2 (2002).

10. bell hooks, *Teaching to Transgress: Education as the Practice of Freedom* (New York: Routledge, 1994), 199.

11. Of course, Michael Apple has given the most thorough analysis of the ideological underpinnings of "official knowledge," see Michael Apple, *Official Knowledge* (New York: Routledge, 2000).

12. hooks, *Teaching to Transgress*, 194.

13. bell hooks, *Teaching Community: A Pedagogy of Hope* (New York: Routledge, 2003), 144.

14. Jane Gallop, *Feminist Accused of Sexual Harassment* (Durham, NC: Duke University Press, 1997).

15. Sigmund Freud, *Group Psychology and the Analysis of the Ego* (New York: W. W. Norton, 1959), 56.

16. For an analysis of the Mary Kay case, see Chapter 6 of Slavoj Zizek, *The Ticklish Subject: The Absent Centre of Political Ontology* (London: Verso, 1999).

17. Sigmund Freud, *Civilization and Its Discontents* (New York: W. W. Norton, 1961).

18. Among the many care theorists, I take as representative of caring pedagogy Nel Noddings and Angela Valenzuela. See Nel Noddings, *Caring: A Feminist Approach to Ethics and Moral Education* (Berkeley: University of California Press, 1984); Angela Valenzuela, *Subtractive Schooling: U.S.-Mexican Youth and the Politics of Caring* (Albany: SUNY Press, 1999). For a particularly revealing account of care, see Tammy A. Shel, *The Ethics of Caring: Bridging Pedagogy and Utopia* (Rotterdam, the Netherlands: Sense, 2007).

19. Valenzuela, *Subtractive Schooling*, 21, emphasis added.

20. Freud, *Group Psychology and the Analysis of the Ego*, 92.

21. Wes Anderson and Owen Wilson, "Rushmore" (Los Angeles: Touchstone, 1998).

22. For more on Lacan and *das Ding* in regard to the neighbor, see Kenneth Reinhard, "Freud, My Neighbor," *American Imago* 54, no. 2 (1997); Kenneth Reinhard, "Kant with Sade, Lacan with Levinas," *Modern Language Notes* 110 (1995).

23. R. Linklater, "School of Rock" (Los Angeles: Paramount, 2003).

24. Jacques Lacan, "The Subversion of the Subject and the Dialectic of Desire in the Freudian Unconscious," in *Écrits: A Selection* (New York and London: W. W. Norton, 2004), 304.
25. This phrase is borrowed from Slavoj Zizek. See Slavoj Zizek, *For They Know Not What They Do: Enjoyment as a Political Factor*, 2nd ed. (London: Verso, 2002), 22. For Lacan's discussion of the day/night signifying system, see (*S* III: 148).
26. California State Board of Education, "Message from the State Board of Education and the State Superindendent of Public Instruction" (Sacramento: CSEA, 2001).
27. Slavoj Zizek, "Class Struggle or Postmodernism? Yes, Please!" in *Contingency, Hegemony, Universality: Contemporary Dialogues on the Left*, ed. Judith Butler, Ernesto Laclau, and Slavoj Zizek (New York: Verso, 2000), 100, original emphasis.
28. Badiou, "What Is Love?" 39, original emphasis.
29. Alain Badiou, "The Scene of Two," *lacanian ink* 21, (Spring/ Summer 2003): 55.
30. Badiou, "What Is Love?" 49.
31. Paulo Freire, *Teachers as Cultural Workers: Letters to Those Who Dare Teach* (Boulder, CO: Westview, 1998), 22, original emphasis.
32. Paulo Freire, *Pedagogy of the Oppressed*, trans. Myra Bergman Ramos (New York and London: Continuum, 1970), 72.
33. Badiou, "What Is Love?" 49.
34. Freire, Teachers as Cultural Workers, 3.

Chapter 8

1. Carl Schmitt, *Political Theology: Four Chapters on the Concept of Sovereignty*, trans. George Schwab (Cambridge, MA: MIT Press, 1985).
2. Walter Benjamin, "Theses on the Philosophy of History," in *Illuminations: Essays and Reflections*, ed. Hannah Arendt (New York: Schocken, 1968), 257.
3. The National Commission on Excellence in Education, "A Nation at Risk: The Imperative for Educational Reform," (1983), http://www.ed.gov/pubs/NatAtRisk/risk.html (retrieved on January 8, 2009).
4. California State Board of Education, "Message from the State Board of Education and the State Superindendent of Public Instruction," (Sacramento: CSEA, 2001).
5. Terry Eagleton, *Literary Theory: An Introduction* (Minneapolis: University of Minnesota Press, 1983), 16.

6. Raymond Williams, *The Long Revolution* (London: Chatto and Windus, 1961).

7. Michael Apple, *Official Knowledge* (New York: Routledge, 2000).

8. Jacques Lacan, "The Subversion of the Subject and the Dialectic of Desire in the Freudian Unconscious," in *Écrits: A Selection* (New York and London: W. W. Norton, 2004).

9. Jacques Lacan, *The Seminar of Jacques Lacan, Book III: The Psychoses, 1955–1956*, trans. Russell Grigg (New York: W. W. Norton, 1993), 148–49.

10. Slavoj Zizek, *For They Know Not What They Do: Enjoyment as a Political Factor,* 2nd ed. (London: Verso, 2002), 22.

11. Do we need to be reminded that knowledge is always someone's knowledge? And thus the exclusion of knowledge and its labeling as "unacademic" is *always* the exclusion of a social group and a labeling of that social group as "unacademic."

12. Louis Althusser, "Ideology and Ideological State Apparatus," in *Lenin and Philosophy and Other Essays* (New York: Monthly Review Press, 2001).

13. Guy Debord, *The Society of the Spectacle*, trans. Donald Nicholson-Smith (New York: Zone, 1995).

14. Douglas Kellner has conducted an important critical analysis of the media's spectacularization of school shootings; see Douglas Kellner, *Guys and Guns Amok: Domestic Terrorism and School Shootings from the Oklahoma City Bombing to the Virginia Tech Massacre* (Boulder, CO: Paradigm, 2008).

15. Michael Moore, "Farenheit 9/11," ed. Michael Moore (Vancouver: Lions Gate, 2004).

16. Julia Kristeva, *Powers of Horror: An Essay on Abjection*, trans. Leon S. Roudiez (New York: Columbia University Press, 1982), 1.

17. Paulo Freire, *Pedagogy of the Oppressed*, trans. Myra Bergman Ramos (New York and London: Continuum, 1970).

18. Irene Costera and Baukje Prins, "How Bodies Come to Matter: An Interview with Judith Butler," *Signs: Journal of Women in Culture and Society* 23, no. 2 (1998): 281.

19. Jacques Ranciere, *Disagreement*, trans. Julie Rose (Minneapolis: University of Minnesota Press, 1999).

20. Ibid., 9.

21. Alain Badiou, *Saint Paul: The Foundation of Universalism* (Stanford, CA: Stanford University Press, 2003).

22. Alain Badiou, *Ethics: An Essay on the Understanding of Evil* (New York: Verso, 2002).

References

Alston, Kal. "Teaching, Philosophy, and *Eros*: Love as a Relation to Truth." *Educational Theory* 41, no. 4 (1991): 385–95.

Althusser, Louis. *The Humanist Controversy and Other Texts.* Translated by Francois Matherson and G. M. Goshgarian. New York and London: Verso, 2003.

———. "Ideology and Ideological State Apparatus." In *Lenin and Philosophy and Other Essays*, 85–126. New York: Monthly Review Press, 2001.

Anderson, Wes, and Owen Wilson. "Rushmore." Los Angeles: Touchstone, 1998.

Aoki, Douglas. "The Thing Never Speaks for Itself: Lacan and the Pedagogical Politics of Clarity." *Harvard Educational Review* 70, no. 3 (2000): 347-69.

Appel, Stephen. *Positioning Subjects: Psychoanalysis and Critical Educational Studies.* Westport, CT: Bergin and Garvey, 1996.

Apple, Michael. *Official Knowledge.* New York: Routledge, 2000.

Badiou, Alain. "Art and Philosophy." *lacanian ink* 17 (Fall 2000): 48–67.

———. *Ethics: An Essay on the Understanding of Evil.* New York: Verso, 2002.

———. *Infinite Thought: Truth and the Return of Philosophy.* Translated by Justin Clemens and Oliver Feltham. New York: Continuum, 2003.

———. "On Love." Los Angeles, 4/24–25/2004 2004.

———. "On the Philosophy of the Open." Los Angeles, 12/11/03 2003.

———. *Saint Paul: The Foundation of Universalism.* Stanford, CA: Stanford University Press, 2003.

———. "The Scene of Two." *lacanian ink* 21 (Spring/Summer 2003): 42–55.

———. "What Is Love?" *Umbr(a)* One (1996): 37–53.

Baez, Benjamin. "Sex Harassment in Schools: The Politics of Law, Power, Sexuality, and Speech." *Educational Theory* 51, no. 1 (2001): 45–62.

Barnard, Suzanne, and Bruce Fink, eds. *Reading Seminar Xx: Lacan's Major Work on Love, Knowledge, and Feminine Sexuality.* Albany: SUNY Press, 2002.

Benjamin, Walter. "Theses on the Philosophy of History." In *Illuminations: Essays and Reflections,* edited by Hannah Arendt, 253–64. New York: Schocken, 1968.

Bingham, Charles. *Authority Is Relational: Rethinking Educational Empowerment.* Albany: SUNY Press, 2008.

———. "On Paulo Freire's Debt to Psychoanalysis: Authority on the Side of Freedom." *Studies in Philosophy and Education* 21 (2002): 447–64.

Boileau, Pierre, and Thomas Narcejac. "Vertigo." Edited by Alfred Hitchcock. Universal Studios, 1958.

Bracher, Mark. *Radical Pedagogy: Identity, Generativity, and Social Transformation.* New York: Palgrave Macmillan, 2006.

———. *The Writing Cure: Psychoanalysis, Composition, and the Aims of Education.* Carbondale and Edwardsville: Southern Illinois University Press, 1999.

Britzman, Deborah. *After-Education: Anna Freud, Melanie Klein, and Psychoanalytic Histories of Learning.* Albany: SUNY Press, 2003.

———. *Lost Subjects, Contested Objects: Toward a Psychoanalytic Inquiry of Learning.* Albany: SUNY Press, 1998.

———. *Novel Education: Psychoanalytic Studies of Learning and Not Learning.* New York and Frakfurt am Main: Peter Lang, 2006.

California State Board of Education. "Message from the State Board of Education and the State Superindendent of Public Instruction." Sacramento: CSEA, 2001.

Caruth, Cathy, ed. *Trauma: Explorations in Memory.* Baltimore and London: Johns Hopkins University Press, 1995.

———. *Unclaimed Experience: Trauma, Narrative and History.* Baltimore and London: Johns Hopkins University Press, 1996.

Cho, Daniel, and Tyson Lewis. "Education and Event: Thinking Radical Pedagogy in an Era of Standardization." *Simile: Studies in Media & Information Literacy Education* 5, no. 2 (2005): article number 62.

Clemens, Justin, and Russell Grigg, eds. *Jacques Lacan and the Other Side of Psychoanalysis: Reflections on Seminar XVII.* Durham, NC: Duke University Press, 2006.

Costera, Irene, and Baukje Prins. "How Bodies Come to Matter: An Interview with Judith Butler." *Signs: Journal of Women in Culture and Society* 23, no. 2 (1998): 275–86.

Debord, Guy. *The Society of the Spectacle.* Translated by Donald Nicholson-Smith. New York: Zone, 1995.

Deleuze, Gilles, and Felix Guattari. *Anti-Oedipus: Capitalism and Schizophrenia.* Minneapolis: Minnesota University Press, 1983.

———. *A Thousand Plateaus.* Minneapolis: University of Minnesota Press, 1987.

Descartes, Rene. *Meditations on First Philosophy.* Translated by John Cottingham. Cambridge and New York: Cambridge University Press, 1986.

Dewey, John. *Democracy and Education.* New York: Free Press, 1997.

Dolar, Mladen. "Beyond Interpellation." *Qui Parle* 6, no. 2, Spring/Summer (1993): 75–96.

Eagleton, Terry. *Literary Theory: An Introduction.* Minneapolis: University of Minnesota Press, 1983.

Eisenstein, Paul. *Traumatic Encounters: Holocaust Representation and the Hegelian Subject.* Albany: SUNY Press, 2003.

Ellsworth, Elizabeth. *Teaching Positions: Difference, Pedagogy, and the Power of Address.* New York: Teachers College Press, 1997.

———. "Why Doesn't This Feel Empowering? Working through the Repressive Myth of Critical Pedagogy." *Harvard Educational Review* 59, no. 3 (1989): 297–324.

Felman, Shoshana. "Education and Crisis, or the Vicissitudes of Teaching." *American Imago* 48, no. 1 (1991): 13–73.

———. "Psychoanalysis and Education: Teaching Terminable and Interminable." *Yale French Studies* 63 (1982): 21–44.

———, and Dori Laub. *Testimony: Crises of Witnessing in Literature, Psychoanalysis, and History.* New York and London: Routledge, 1992.

Fink, Bruce. *A Clinical Introduction to Lacanian Psychoanalysis.* Cambridge, MA: Harvard University Press, 1997.

———. *The Lacanian Subject.* Princeton, NJ: Princeton University Press, 1995.

———, Maire Jaanus, and Richard Feldstein, eds. *Reading Seminar I and II: Lacan's Return to Freud.* Albany: SUNY Press, 1996.

———, Maire Jaanus, and Richard Feldstein, eds. *Reading Seminar XI: Lacan's Four Fundamental Concepts of Psychoanalysis.* Albany: SUNY Press, 1995.

Foucault, Michel. *Order of Things: An Archaeology of the Human Sciences.* New York: Routledge, 2001.

Freire, Paulo. "The Adult Literacy Process as Cultural Action for Freedom." *Harvard Educational Review* 68, no. 4 (1998): 480–98.

———. "Cultural Action for Freedom." *Harvard Educational Review* 68, no. 4 (1998): 471–521.

———. *Pedagogy of Freedom: Ethics, Democracy, and Civic Courage.* Translated by Patrick Clarke. Lanham, MD: Rowman and Littlefield, 1998.

———. *Pedagogy of Hope.* New York: Continuum, 2003.

———. *Pedagogy of the Oppressed.* Translated by Myra Bergman Ramos. New York and London: Continuum, 1970.

———. *The Politics of Education: Culture, Power and Liberation.* Westport, CT: Bergin and Garvey, 1984.

———. *Teachers as Cultural Workers: Letters to Those Who Dare Teach.* Boulder, CO: Westview, 1998.

Freud, Anna. *Psychoanalysis for Teachers and Parents.* New York: W. W. Norton, 1979.

Freud, Sigmund. *Civilization and Its Discontents.* New York: W. W. Norton, 1961.

———. *Dora: An Analysis of a Case of Hysteria.* New York: Touchstone, 1963.

———. *Group Psychology and the Analysis of the Ego.* New York: Norton, 1959.

———. *The Psychopathology of Everyday Life.* Translated by James Strachey. New York and London: W. W. Norton, 1965.

———. *The Standard Edition of the Complete Psychological Works of Sigmund Freud.* Translated and edited by James Strachey. 24 vols. London: Hogarth, 1953–74.

———. *The Uncanny.* Translated by Hugh Haughton. New York: Penguin, 2003.

———. *The "Wolfman" and Other Cases.* In *The New Penguin Freud.* Translated by Louise Adey Huish. Edited by Adam Phillips. New York: Penguin, 2003.

———, and Josef Breuer. *Studies in Hysteria.* Translated by Nicola Luckhurst. New York and London: Penguin, 2004.

Gallop, Jane. *Feminist Accused of Sexual Harassment.* Durham, NC: Duke University Press, 1997.

Giroux, Henry. *Border Crossings: Cultural Workers and the Politics of Education.* New York and London: Routledge, 2005.

———. *Theory and Resistance in Education: Towards a Pedagogy for the Opposition.* Westport, CT: Bergin and Garvey, 1983.

———, and Patrick Shannon, eds. *Education and Cultural Studies: Toward a Performative Practice.* New York and London: Routledge, 1997.

Hallward, Peter. *Badiou: A Subject to Truth.* Minneapolis: University of Minnesota Press, 2003.

hooks, bell. *Teaching Community: A Pedagogy of Hope.* New York: Routledge, 2003.

———. *Teaching to Transgress: Education as the Practice of Freedom.* New York: Routledge, 1994.

Huffaker, Donna. "Teacher Pleads Not Guilty in Sex Case; Judge Rejects Bid to Lower Granda Hills High Instructor's Bail." *Daily News of Los Angeles,* March 17, 1999.

jagodzinski, jan. *Music in Youth Culture: A Lacanian Approach.* New York: Palgrave Macmillan, 2005.

———, ed. *Pedagogical Desire: Authority, Seduction, Transference, and the Question of Ethics.* Westport, CT: Bergin and Garvey, 2002.

———. *Television and Youth Culture: Televised Paranoia.* New York: Palgrave Macmillan, 2008.

———. *Youth Fantasies: The Perverse Landscape of the Media.* New York: Palgrave Macmillan, 2004.

Kellner, Douglas. *Guys and Guns Amok: Domestic Terrorism and School Shootings from the Oklahoma City Bombing to the Virginia Tech Massacre.* Boulder, CO: Paradigm, 2008.

Kincheloe, Joe L., and William F. Pinar, eds. *Curriculum as Social Psychoanalysis: The Significance of Place.* Albany: SUNY Press, 1991.

Kornbluh, Anna. "For the Love of Money." *Historical Materialism* 10, no. 4 (2002): 155–71.

Kristeva, Julia. *Powers of Horror: An Essay on Abjection.* Translated by Leon S. Roudiez. New York: Columbia University Press, 1982.

Lacan, Jacques. *Écrits: The First Complete Edition in English.* Translated by Bruce Fink. New York: W. W. Norton, 2007.

———. "The Instance of the Letter in the Unconscious, or Reason since Freud." In *Écrits: A Selection,* 138–68. New York and London: W. W. Norton, 2002.

———. "The Mirror Stage as Formative of the Function of the I." In *Écrits: A Selection,* 3–9. New York and London: W. W. Norton, 2004.

————. "Science and Truth." *Newsletter of the Freudian Field* 3 (1989): 4–29.

————. *The Seminar of Jacques Lacan, Book I: Freud's Papers on Technique, 1953–1954.* Translated by John Forrester. New York: W. W. Norton, 1988.

————. *The Seminar of Jacques Lacan, Book II: The Ego in Freud's Theory and in the Technique of Psychoanalysis, 1954–1955.* Translated by Sylvana Tomaselli. New York: W. W. Norton, 1991.

————. *The Seminar of Jacques Lacan, Book III: The Psychoses, 1955–1956.* Translated by Russell Grigg. New York: Norton, 1993.

————. *The Seminar of Jacques Lacan, Book VII: The Ethics of Psychoanalysis.* Translated by Dennis Porter. New York: Norton, 1992.

————. *The Seminar of Jacques Lacan, Book XI: The Four Fundamental Concepts of Psychoanalysis.* Translated by Alan Sheridan. Edited by Jacques-Alain Miller. New York and London: W. W. Norton, 1981.

————. *The Seminar of Jacques Lacan, Book XVII: The Other Side of Psychoanalysis.* Translated by Russell Grigg. New York: W. W. Norton, 2007.

————. *The Seminar of Jacques Lacan, Book XX: Encore: On Feminine Sexuality, the Limits of Love and Knowledge.* Translated by Bruce Fink. New York: Norton, 1988.

————. "The Subversion of the Subject and the Dialectic of Desire in the Freudian Unconscious." In *Écrits: A Selection*, 281–312. New York and London: W. W. Norton, 2004.

LaCapra, Dominick. *History and Memory after Auschwitz.* Ithaca, NY Cornell University Press, 1998.

————. *Writing History, Writing Trauma.* Baltimore and London: Johns Hopkins University Press, 2000.

Lather, Patti. "Critical Pedagogy and Its Complicities: A Praxis of Stuck Places." *Educational Theory* 48, no. 4 (1998): 487–97.

Laurent, Eric. "Alienation and Separation (I)." In *Reading Seminar XI: Lacan's Four Fundamental Concepts of Psychoanalysis*, edited by Richard Feldstein, Bruce Fink, and Maire Jaanus, 19–28. Albany: SUNY Press, 1995.

Leys, Ruth. *Trauma: A Genealogy.* Chicago: Chicago University Press, 2000.

Linklater, Richard. *School of Rock*: Paramount, 2003.

Lukacs, Georg. *History and Class Consciousness.* Cambridge, MA: MIT Press, 1968.

Luke, Carmen, and Jennifer Gore, eds. *Feminisms and Critical Pedagogy.* New York and London: Routledge, 1992.

Markham, Mick. "Through the Looking Glass: Reflective Teaching through a Lacanian Lens." *Curriculum Inquiry* 29, no. 1 (1999): 55–76.

Marx, Karl. *Capital.* Translated by Ben Fowkes. Vol. 1. New York: Penguin, 1990.

McLaren, Peter. *Critical Pedagogy and Predatory Culture.* New York and London: Routledge, 1995.

———. *Life in Schools: An Introduction to Critical Pedagogy in the Foundations of Education.* Needham Heights, MA: Allyn and Bacon, 1998.

Mill, John Stuart. "Class Struggle and Mode of Production." In *The Marx-Engels Reader*, edited by Robert C. Tucker, 220. New York and London: W. W. Norton, 1978.

———. *On Liberty.* Arlington Heights, IL: AHM, 1947.

———. "Wage Labour and Capital." In *The Marx-Engels Reader*, edited by Robert C. Tucker, 203–17. New York: W. W. Norton, 1978.

Moi, Toril. "From Femininity to Finitude: Freud, Lacan, and Feminism, Again." *Signs: Journal of Women in Culture and Society* 29, no. 3 (2004): 841–78.

Moore, Michael. "Farenheit 9/11." Edited by Michael Moore. Vancouver: Lions Gate, 2004.

Morris, Marla. *Curriculum and the Holocaust: Competing Sites of Memory and Representation.* New York: Lawrence Erlbaum, 2001

National Commission on Excellence in Education, The. "A Nation at Risk: The Imperative for Educational Reform." 1983.

Noddings, Nel. *Caring: A Feminist Approach to Ethics and Moral Education.* Berkeley: University of California Press, 1984.

Nolan, Christopher, and Jonathan Nolan. *Memento.* Edited by Christopher Nolan. Sony Pictures, 2000.

Payne, A. "Election." Los Angeles: Paramount, 1999.

Pitt, Alice. *The Play of the Personal: Psychoanalytic Narratives of Feminist Education.* New York and Frankfurt am Main: Peter Lang, 2003.

———, Judith P. Robertson, and Sharon Todd, eds. *Special Issue on Psychoanalysis.* Vol. 14, *Jct: Journal of Curriculum Theorizing,* 1998.

Ranciere, Jacques. *Disagreement.* Translated by Julie Rose. Minneapolis: University of Minnesota Press, 1999.

———. *The Ignorant Schoolmaster: Five Lessons in Intellectual Emancipation.* Translated by Kristin Ross. Stanford, CA: Stanford University Press, 1991.

Reinhard, Kenneth. "Freud, My Neighbor." *American Imago* 54, no. 2 (1997): 165–95.

———. "Kant with Sade, Lacan with Levinas." *Modern Language Notes* 110 (1995): 785–808.

Roseboro, Donyell. *Jacques Lacan and Education: A Critical Introduction.* Rotterdam: Sense, 2008.

Rothberg, Michael. *Traumatic Realism: The Demands of Holocaust Representation.* Minneapolis: University of Minnesota Press, 2000.

Samuels, Robert. *Teaching the Rhetoric of Resistance: The Popular Holocaust and Social Change in a Post 9/11 World.* New York: Palgrave Macmillan, 2007.

Sartre, Jean-Paul. *Critique of Dialectical Reason.* Vol. 1 Translated by Alan Sheridan-Smith. New York and London: Verso, 2004

Schmitt, Carl. *Political Theology: Four Chapters on the Concept of Sovereignty.* Translated by George Schwab. Cambridge, MA: MIT Press, 1985.

Shel, Tammy A. *The Ethics of Caring: Bridging Pedagogy and Utopia.* Rotterdam, the Netherlands: Sense, 2007.

Simpson, Timothy, and James Scott Johnston. "*Eros* between Plato and Garrison: Recovering Lost Desire." *Educational Theory* 52, no. 2 (2002): 223–39.

Todd, Sharon, ed. *Learning Desire: Perspectives on Pedagogy, Culture, and the Unsaid.* New York: Routledge, 1997.

———. *Learning from the Other: Levinas, Psychoanalysis, and Ethical Possibilities in Education.* Albany: SUNY Press, 2003.

Valenzuela, Angela. *Subtractive Schooling: U.S.-Mexican Youth and the Politics of Caring.* Albany: SUNY Press, 1999.

Weiss, Lisa, and Donna Huffaker. "Teacher Held as Suspect in Teen Sex Case." *Daily News of Los Angeles,* March 15, 1999.

Williams, Raymond. *The Long Revolution.* London: Chatto and Windus, 1961.

Zizek, Slavoj. "Class Struggle or Postmodernism? Yes, Please!" In *Contingency, Hegemony, Universality: Contemporary Dialogues on the Left.* Edited by Judith Butler, Ernesto Laclau, and Slavoj Zizek, 90–135. New York: Verso, 2000.

————, ed. *Cogito and the Unconscious*. Durham, NC: Duke University Press, 1998.

————. *Did Somebody Say Totalitarianism? Five Interventions in the (Mis)Use of a Notion*. New York: Verso, 2002.

————. *Iraq: The Borrowed Kettle*. New York and London: Verso, 2005.

————. *Revolution at the Gates: Zizek on Lenin, the 1917 Writings*. New York and London: Verso, 2002.

————. *The Sublime Object of Ideology*. New York: Verso, 1989.

————. *For They Know Not What They Do: Enjoyment as a Political Factor*. 2nd ed. London: Verso, 2002.

————. The Ticklish Subject: The Absent Centre of Political Ontology. London: Verso, 1999.

Index